Advanced Writing Skills
for Students of English

Phil Williams

Copyright

Cover design by Phil Williams

Cover images © DavidArts, © schiva (Depositphotos)

ISBN: 978-0-9931808-5-9

Published by English Lessons Brighton, an imprint of Rumian Publishing

Contents

Introduction

This book is aimed at helping foreign learners of English improve their writing skills, though the tips included can help anyone with an interest in English. These tips are approached from a technical viewpoint of the English language, with consideration of grammar and structural rules. My intention is to provide a bridge between a solid understanding of English and more fluent and effective use of the language in writing. Through learning and applying the contents of this book, you may develop your writing as a skill, with an appreciation for style and technique that goes beyond the standard rules.

Some of these tips are specific to a style that I personally believe works, and are intended to objectively improve general writing. At a certain level, any writer must develop their own style. You may find conflicting viewpoints elsewhere, which I encourage you to study too. I have tried, to the best of my ability, to explain why the advice I offer makes a difference, so you may decide for yourself if it makes sense for you. A book cannot improve your skills on its own, though, just as a book cannot make you good at sports. This guide can only help you develop your skills yourself. Real improvement will come from practice.

I believe there are three key ways to improve your writing, which you cannot neglect:

1. Read more
2. Write more
3. Study more

Read more, in this context, means read examples of other writing in use. By reading what others have written (good or bad), you will discover unusual words, styles and structures. When you observe these and question why they do or do not work, you will develop the ability to use them yourself. When you **write more**, you then have better resources to develop a personal style that works for you. **Study** is necessary when you need to fill the gap between these two areas, when there are elements of the writing craft that are not easily understood through observation, or that need extra understanding.

The purpose of this guide is to provide an understanding of such areas; to fill in the details that might not be immediately obvious in your own reading and writing. I hope to give you answers concerning why and how different techniques are used, so that you might use (or avoid using) them yourself.

The lessons in this book can benefit both foreign learners and native English speakers. Many English speakers reach adulthood and stop writing, except on rare occasions, and, as with any unused skill, it can then become more difficult. Whether or not English is your native tongue, employing the lessons of this guide can therefore take you beyond the average level of English writing skills. Your challenge is to constantly question English usage, to learn why certain technical rules are important and how styles can vary. By analysing these areas, you will develop the ability to use them yourself. You may also develop a keen sense for bad practices and mistakes.

In the spirit of questioning everything, a good place to start is explaining where the content of this book comes from. The rules in this book are informed by grammar and style guides, but the tips come from my own application of these ideas. I have a background in teaching English as a foreign language, in schools and through private tutoring. Tutoring particularly allowed me to focus on the finer details of individuals' language use. To explore and explain advanced English usage, I deconstructed the language together with my students. I combined this with my personal passion for writing. I started writing creatively at a very early age. I write novels, business texts, articles teaching English and educational books, amongst other things. Alongside my tutoring work, I have used my writing skills to edit texts for people across an even wider field. Many of my students have asked how I do it. This book is my attempt to explain some of the theory behind a skill that was learnt through practice, so it may, hopefully, provide shortcuts for others to follow.

I encourage you to apply the lessons of this book for yourself, to see what works for you. It is a lifelong interest for me to continue learning about the English language, as I hope it is for you, and I encourage active reading of this book. If something in here does not make sense to you, do send me an email (my details are at the back of the book). There is likely to be a good reason for it.

How to Use This Book

Advanced Writing Skills for Students of English has been written as a series of discussion essays. It covers the topics that I feel are most relevant and useful for improving general writing skills (Part 1), followed by brief tips for specific areas of writing (Part 2). You can use this book as a reference guide, going straight to the sections that most interest you, or it can be read in a linear way, from start to finish.

As style is referenced throughout the book, it's worth noting some of the specific styles I have chosen to use myself:

- *Italics* show examples within the main text, book titles, or commentary within listed and quoted examples.
- Bullet points are used to indicate most examples, as seen here, but longer examples are shown as block quotes, separated from the main text.
- **Bold** is used to show rules, to highlight specific words, or to emphasise words within an example.
- Chapters are used to explore main themes, with sub-chapters and sub-headings for more specific ideas.

This book contains references to other books, citing surname and year, with the full references available in the **Recommended Reading** section. References are also made to other chapters, numbered and in bold.

This book covers writing from many different fields, variously referred to as **non-fiction** (e.g. factual writing, academic, business, correspondence) and **fiction** (e.g. creative writing, novels, stories). You may choose to focus on the areas that are most applicable to you, but I recommend studying other fields of writing, too, as it will hone different, transferrable skills.

Please note that this book is written in British English and follows UK style conventions, though it is intended for readers all over the world. Although consideration has been given to the differences between British and American English, it may contain regionally specific language.

Part 1

General Writing

1. Style

Language skills like writing are called **skills** because they require practice and nuanced understanding. Using English at an advanced level is not as simple as learning rules: it can be flexible, regionally specific or individual. In writing, many of these areas can be grouped under the label **style**.

The way we use style is subjective. Consider this dictionary definition:

> **Style:** a particular procedure by which something is done; a manner or a way. (*Oxford Living Dictionaries*)

This includes the way you use language. If there are two (or more) ways to do something in writing, it may be considered **a matter of style**. I often use this expression when teaching, and it appears throughout this book. When you have a choice in how to write something, or when a different way of saying something cannot be called incorrect, for any objective reason, it may be called a matter of style.

To be clear about what is **not** a matter of style, some errors, such as grammar or spelling mistakes, may be clearly incorrect:

- Tim eats a cake yesterday. *(INCORRECT – it is contradictory to combine the present tense with a past time.)*
- Tim ate a cake yesterday. *(CORRECT)*

With a matter of style, the different options should both be arguably correct:

- Bob quickly ate a cake yesterday.
- Bob ate a cake yesterday, quickly.

The first example here is more conventional and more common, but the second form is also acceptable. There may be a handful of reasons to use the second sentence over the first, which we could analyse, but there may also be no reason other than the writer or speaker chose to say it this way, without necessarily thinking about it. In writing, such style choices go beyond what you wish to say to include how things are technically written, covering issues relating to formatting, punctuation, vocabulary, grammar and more.

Style choices are very important because there are so many elements of the language that are flexible. Many choices must be decided by style rather than any easily applied rules. The differences between academic or business writing, or regional uses of English, are all matters of style. They are not objectively correct or incorrect, but fit a particular purpose. That said, flexible use of English is less forgiving in writing than in spoken English. People may not notice or correct variations in spoken English, as physical and social cues aid understanding, but people read in more neutral tones and expect a higher level of accuracy in writing. To really advance in writing, as well as mastering the conventional rules of English, you therefore also need to understand which style choices are acceptable or advisable in different circumstances. This might be decided through convention, for example the stock phrases used when starting letters, or it may be through a particular set of rules, such as given in a style guide.

Style guides are collections of rules that cover the many areas of English that might be considered flexible. Their purpose is to provide consistency. There is no definitive, correct style for English, so there are plenty of style guides to choose from. Of the published guides available, a popular starting point for UK styles is *New Hart's Rules: the Oxford Style Guide* (Waddingham, 2014), while for US styles you might start with *The Chicago Manual of Style* (University of Chicago, 2017). *The Elements of Style* (Strunk & White, 1999), is another slim but informative example, which has been used in the United States since the early twentieth century. While such books are invaluable for publications, they are not used by everyone. Many companies and institutions (such as universities or government offices) maintain their own in-house style guides, with rules that all employees should follow. These are not necessarily standard English rules, though they will typically be commonly used.

However you choose to settle your style decisions, there are three crucial things you can do to ensure an appropriate style:

1. Use a style that is clear and accurate.
2. Use a style that fits the purpose of your writing.
3. Be consistent.

For **clarity and accuracy**, choose the style that is easiest to understand. To **fit the purpose of your writing**, compare with other examples of writing in the same field, and consider the tips throughout this book as to where one style may be expected over another. For **consistency**, use the same style throughout a document.

While styles can be subjective, ignoring these three points could still lead to a mistake. Possible style options that are correct out of context may become incorrect when applied in a specific context. For example:

- Using complicated language to provide simple instructions.
- Using slang in a formal letter.
- Using both apostrophes and quotation marks to denote speech.

The use of complex language, slang and quotation marks are all possible in written English, if you choose to use them, but in the examples above they could be considered incorrect. The first is unclear, the second inappropriate and the third inconsistent.

To start thinking more constructively about style, it is important to always be asking why something is written in a certain way, and if that is the best way to do it. When you see something unusual in your reading, ask yourself if it is a matter of style, and if so, why? What is its purpose? When you are writing, ask yourself the same questions. If you are presented with a choice, ask what difference each choice makes, and try to justify your reasons for choosing one option over another.

This book is not a style guide, but it gives you some of the general patterns and rules that can help you make style decisions. Rather than focus on one style over another, my intention is to encourage an understanding of the differences, to help you choose for yourself. That being said, you may notice within this book that certain style choices have been made, and one thing I support throughout, which could be considered a style choice, is clear and simple writing. Such choices are ones that I have found helped me, and which I will attempt to justify, starting with the following chapter.

2. Simplicity

There is a rule that is taught in almost all settings of writing, which is helpful whatever the purpose of your writing.

Keep It Simple

This is usually presented in a memorable acronym: **KISS** (in its complete form, *Keep It Simple, Stupid*, but there's no need to be negative). Many writing tips have roots in this idea. Simple language is clearer for the reader and easier for the writer. Simple structures avoid confusion and complications.

Simplicity needs to be considered at every stage of your writing. It can come before planning, even. When it seems difficult to start a piece of writing, using the simplest approach makes it easier. Start with the one point you want your writing to say. Continue with the simplest way to say it.

Keeping your language simple is the basic foundation of effective writing. Simple writing is direct and agreeable. It is also easier to write without mistakes. Do not give in to the temptation to make things complicated!

2.1 Why Complicate Life?

When you learn more, there is a temptation to use everything you have learnt, including new words, new structures, and new ideas. There are two problems with this. First, what is new to you may also be new to someone else, and therefore difficult to understand. Second, advanced language is not necessarily clear language, as complex words and structures can easily become long-winded and difficult to read.

Some contexts demand more complex language, such as in academic papers and when exploring complex or specialist topics. In exam settings, you may also be expected to demonstrate a varied and complicated use of language. In real world usage, however, complex and advanced language may actually make communication harder. Even in academic and specialist texts, simple language is advisable wherever possible, to make complicated ideas clearer.

Knowing **when** to use advanced language can only come through a proper understanding of **how** and **why** it is used. Difficult words and structures often exist to suit specific circumstances. Consider how we describe colours: a full spectrum of words exists to label different blues, such as *azure*, *sapphire*, and *navy blue*. There's even a blue called *phthalo*. If a very particular shade is important, then the specific word is important. If we simply want to distinguish between something that is broadly different, the simpler word is better, as it is most likely to be understood. Consider these examples:

- All bridesmaids must wear sapphire dresses so they match.
- We own two cars – mine's the blue one, not the red one.

In the first example, the specific shade is important to distinguish from other blues. In the second sentence, the specific shade is not important as we are distinguishing from red.

This simple example could be applied to all areas of language. Use as much detail as is necessary and no more. Your writing will then be as complicated as it needs to be without being too complicated.

2.2 How to Keep It Simple

It is possible to consciously avoiding writing anything too complicated. Write short, simple sentences, one idea at a time. Use the most simple language. You can add more complex language later, if you decide it is needed.

Starting simple can require a lot of thought and feel unnatural, though. The alternative is to write however you feel, with whatever words and constructions come to mind, then **edit ruthlessly**. Complete your writing without worrying about its quality or complexity, then remove or change everything that is not necessary. Many great writers in English repeat this tip: the key to shorter, simpler writing is editing and cutting. Novelist Stephen

King famously recommended removing about 10% of your writing with each redraft (King, *On Writing*, 2010). The actual number is not important, but the principle is solid. Shorter writing is forced to be simpler.

Careful editing will encourage you to approach complicated language with a sense of purpose. It makes it easier to understand when such language is appropriate, and the lessons you learn from editing will become part of your natural writing.

For a more specific path towards simple writing, consider George Orwell's advice for writing in practice, published in his essay *Politics and the English Language* (1946):

1. Never use a metaphor, simile, or other figure of speech which you are used to seeing in print.
2. Never use a long word where a short one will do.
3. If it is possible to cut a word out, always cut it out.
4. Never use the passive where you can use the active.
5. Never use a foreign phrase, a scientific word, or a jargon word if you can think of an everyday English equivalent.
6. Break any of these rules sooner than say anything outright barbarous.

With the exception of point 6, all of these tips are designed to simplify your writing and remove complicated or unclear language. Tip 6, however, refers to the choices that must be made when complicated language and constructions are necessary. For more detailed discussion of Orwell's ideas, consider reading his entire essay, which is available online (see **Recommended Reading** for a link). These principles are also covered in more detail later in this book.

3. Planning

Good writing starts before you write a single word. Preparing what you are about to write, whether in your head or with an actual plan, makes writing easier and more effective.

The more comfortable you are with writing, the less planning you may need, but good planning makes writing easier at all levels. Preparation should also reduce how much time you need to spend editing.

How you plan your writing will depend on your specific project and preference. Some techniques you can use include brainstorming (writing all the ideas you can think of at once) or mind mapping (putting your ideas on cards or a computer program and moving them around). For certain pieces of writing, such as an IELTS (International English Language Testing System) exam or a standardised report, you may be able to plan using a particular template, for example listing Intro, Paragraph 1, Paragraph 2, etc. It is important to find a method that best helps you organise your writing.

A useful starting point can be to answer a series of questions that establish your subject matter and the tone of your writing. These questions should be relevant for all writers of all abilities, in all areas:

1. What's the purpose of your writing?
2. Who are you writing for?
3. What structure will you use?
4. What style will you use?
5. How will you conclude?

3.1 What's the Purpose of Your Writing?

A solid understanding of **why** you are writing provides focus. Start with looking for one, clear purpose. When you know the purpose of your writing, you can check that every paragraph, and every sentence, is necessary. Sentences or words that do not help your purpose dilute your point, which

13

can weaken your writing or lead to confusion or boredom. Remove any unnecessary writing. This helps keep your writing clear and simple.

Be careful to actually identify a **purpose** for your writing, not simply a subject. A specific purpose helps guide specific language and ideas. Consider these possible responses to an essay task *Write an essay about green energy*:

- "I will write what I know about green energy."
- "I will explain the benefits of green energy."
- "I will argue that green energy can improve the environment."

The first response provides a general subject without a purpose, so it lacks focus. It gives us no clear start or end. The second example is an improvement, as we have a better idea of where to begin, but still doesn't tell us why. Only the third, which is most specific, gives us a clear idea of **why** we are writing, and therefore where we want our writing to go. This response immediately conjures the need to explore examples of environmental problems and how green energy can impact them. By deciding to argue a point from the start, we also know the sort of language and constructions that will be required.

To decide upon a clear purpose for your writing, think of an action you wish your reader to take, or an attitude you wish them to adopt. This can apply to the simplest modes of writing, such as a text message aiming to amuse a friend, through to the most complex documents, such as a research paper designed to influence a change in government policy.

3.2 Who Are You Writing For?

All writing should be aimed at a particular reader. Picture your ideal, or most likely reader, and you can plan the points and language that will have the most impact on them. This will help you make decisions on how simple or complicated you make the text, what sort of argument you make, and how you phrase your arguments. An email to an employer, for example, should be prepared differently to an email to a friend. Similarly, an academic book written for other academics may be written differently to an academic book intended for the public.

Defining your audience will give you focus, setting limitations on what you write. Text length, vocabulary, and key points can all be adjusted according to a specific idea of who you are writing for. When you have decided exactly who will read the text, you can better test how effectively your writing fits its purpose.

3.3 What Structure Will You Use?

Good structure makes writing more effective.

This may seem obvious in exam settings and with texts that follow particular conventions, such as cover letters or essays. It may be less obvious, however, that structure is equally important in less restrictive writing, such as in emails or creative writing.

A planned structure can help you set targets and develop an overall sense of rhythm for your writing. Carefully consider the length and order of the points you intend to make. This will help the writing flow and prevent you from writing too much or from introducing ideas in the wrong place. A sensible structure moves the writing along logically, making it easier both to write and for others to read. Effective structure can also help engage your reader, while poor structure can be distracting and unclear. Effective structure is covered in more detail in the following chapter, **4. Structure**.

3.4 What Style Will You Use?

Once you have an idea of why you are writing, who you are writing for, and the structure of your writing, the words can flow. At this point you still have to make choices, though. How formal or informal should you be? Should you write in long paragraphs, short sentences, first person, a particular tense? What spelling conventions or regional vocabulary are acceptable?

If you want to write in a certain style, always ask yourself why before you begin. It is more difficult to change styles after you have already started.

As discussed in **1. Style**, full consideration of style is perhaps the most complex part of mastering the English language, not only in writing. This is because so many language rules depend on context and decision-based situations, and cannot be applied universally. Throughout this book you will find examples of this, with explanations of why you might opt for some styles over others. These are decisions best made early on, and can be best decided when you can ask yourself what language will fit the purpose and audience you have defined.

3.5 How Will You Conclude?

Knowing how to end any piece of writing can be the single most powerful tool in getting you started. It is strongly connected to the purpose of your writing: if you know why you are writing, your conclusion or call to action should be clear. This gives you something to work towards, and focuses all of your writing on reaching that point. It is easier to move forwards when you know where you are going, after all.

Consider these examples, where the added focus of a clear conclusion or ending should make the text easier to imagine:

- Write an essay on the pros and cons of electric showers.
  → Write an essay concluding that electric showers are bad because they are expensive.
- Write a story about a medieval knight.
  → Write a story that ends with a medieval knight dying to protect the woman he loves.

Giving your writing a clear purpose may provide a clear ending immediately. If not, you may need to rethink your purpose, and how you would like to impact the reader. This will guide what you write and how you write it.

Perhaps equally importantly, a strong idea of how you wish to finish provides motivation to get to the end.

4. Structure

Structure is important at all levels of writing, from the order of words in sentences through to the order that you present information. This starts with the understanding that you need a beginning, a middle and an end in everything you write.

A standard sentence can begin with a subject, followed by a verb, ending with an object. A letter can begin with a salutation, followed by a message, ending with a valediction. An essay or report can begin with an introduction, followed by the body, then a conclusion. In a piece of creative writing, you may find an inciting incident, a journey and a finale.

Good structure is important for one main reason: it effectively engages the reader. Writing reads more fluently when it hits certain beats, like music. Information presented in an expected order (or an order that aids comprehension or the reading experience) better captures the reader's attention. Incorrect word order or uneven paragraphing can break a reader's attention, and may lead to confusion.

This is not a simple subject. This chapter provides general principles that will help you to start thinking about structure more effectively, whatever your field or purpose. Part 2 gives an introduction to some more specific areas of writing, with further consideration of structure. However, the exact requirements of good structure depend on your subject matter, and whole books exist to help with structuring academic writing, business writing, and creative writing.

Studies have been done into what works in all these areas, not based on language rules but on reader-response and psychology. For examples of how much detail you might need for writing in specific fields, consider books like *Writing That Works* (Roman & Raphaelson, 2000), covering business writing; the classic *The Hero with a Thousand Faces* (Campbell, 2008), for the universal structures of myths; or *Wired for Story* (Cron, 2012), which discusses how specifically paced writing affects the brain.

4.1 Breaking Writing Down

It is useful to break down the structure of your writing, with different scales, to explore how it functions. For example, a piece of writing may have an introduction, discussion, and conclusion. Each section can in turn be broken down into paragraphs. Your paragraphs can be broken down into sentences, and your sentences into component parts. At every level, each part of your writing has its own purpose. When you map out your structures in this way, you can consider the best order before you begin writing, or when editing.

For example, when you write an essay or report with many points, by summarising each point (at least in your mind) you can see how they relate to each other, and can therefore plot a logical order for them. Consider writing a report on the effectiveness of a new product. You might come up with the following four points to begin with:

1. Affordable price
2. Unappealing appearance
3. Excellent functionality
4. Existing customer base

These points currently follow no logical order. By considering this before writing, you can decide on a sensible narrative. You might ask the purpose of each point before connecting them. You could then, for example, start with the positives of the functionality to show the product works, followed by affordable price and existing customer base, for additional positives, before finishing with the one contrasting negative, its appearance.

On a finer level, your paragraphs may also be broken down and seen as component parts (such as positive and negative sentences within a point), and likewise a sentence can be divided into sections with particular purposes. For example, if you wished to emphasise the time in a sentence, you could divide the sentence into two parts and then reorder, moving the time phrase before the rest of the sentence:

- [We went to the church] [at night].
  → [At night,] [we went to the church.]

At this level of detail, sentences can be broken down in a variety of ways depending on your purpose. The functions of clauses and phrases, or specific words like nouns and verbs, may all be more or less important depending on what you want to do with your sentence. The point, though, is that this analysis can help you look at your writing in a structural way, to better organise your message. (Specific techniques for this are covered in **5. Building Sentences** and **6. Paragraphs**).

4.2 Presenting Information at the Right Time

As well as identifying a logical order for your writing, you must also consider when specific information will be most effective, or alternatively when it will be distracting and ineffective. Consider the different reading experience for these two examples:

- He gave her his ex-wife's ring.
- He gave her a ring. It had belonged to his ex-wife.

Neither of these sentences is necessarily correct or incorrect; the different structures suit different purposes. The first example is a fairly neutral statement, open to interpretation. The second example is written for dramatic effect: by presenting the information about the ring as a statement on its own, it gives it particular significance.

Considering how and when you present specific information, you can prepare the reader and provide cues to help your writing flow. You may wish to define difficult terms or concepts before leading into discussion of them, or you may need to put key, framing information earlier than usual in a sentence. You may, on the other hand, avoid presenting information too early, to avoid ruining a twist. Withholding information can also add suspense or surprises. Whatever the case, such structural deviations should always be intentional. The challenge is to present information in its most effective position.

For well-structured, and well-timed, writing, consider the reading experience. Reading is very different to writing, as the reader does not start with the same information as the writer, so a reader might not fully understand a point until a particular moment in your writing. Try to consider what it would be like to read your writing with no advance knowledge. Does it make sense if you don't know what's coming? The effect of this is not only limited to aiding the reader's understanding: it can affect credibility or flow if unexpected information is revealed with no prior warning. If you include surprises in your writing, such as a twist in a story, there should be certain signposts beforehand, to avoid breaking the flow.

4.3 Repeating Information

Repetition can occur with words, phrases, or even whole ideas being repeated. A single principle can be applied to all repetition in writing: you need a particular reason to repeat information. Unnecessary repetition can dilute or muddle your writing, or create a bland reading experience.

If you need to repeat information in your writing, it is often because something is out of place. When you find you have included the same information more than once, consider both instances. Is each instance necessary? Can they be combined, or removed? Why is there repetition at that particular point?

There can, of course, be good reasons for repeated information. This is particularly true in longer writing projects, when used for emphasis, or for consolidating certain vocabulary. However, if you do use repetition, make sure you know the reasons, so it is done by conscious choice.

More help is given for avoiding unintentional word repetition in **7.4 Avoiding Repetition**, whilst intentional, emphatic repetition is covered in **14.4 Repetition for Emphasis**.

5. Building Sentences

Sentences can be broken down and discussed in many different ways, for example as word types (noun, verb, adjective, etc.); as functioning components (subject, verb, object); or as grammatical structures (phrases, clauses). Whichever way you look at a sentence, strong writing starts with accurate structure. Correct basic word order and sentence structure are essential before you can start rearranging sentences to suit the purposes of your writing.

Ordinary word order and sentence structure follow expected patterns. Generally, the subject comes first, then the subject's activity and any object it affects, followed by additional information. The following table gives an example of how sentence components are ordered:

Subject	Verb (s)	Indirect Object	Direct Object	Prepositional phrase	Time
She	gave	him	her book	in the park	yesterday.

This could be adapted to look at specific word types, for typical order, but almost any part of a sentence can be moved through a variety of different techniques, to add emphasis or present information at a deliberate time.

These techniques can give you a great deal of flexibility compared to standard sentence structure and word order, but take practice and skill to do properly. Always be aware that you need a particular reason to deviate from regular structure, which is the most natural and commonly understood form. You may add variety and emphasis, but non-standard order can also make your sentences difficult to follow.

The following sections give some starting points for rethinking the general conventions. Additional help with using and adapting basic sentence structure is also available in my book *Word Order in English Sentences*.

5.1 Starting Sentences

One of the main ways that word order is adjusted is to start a sentence with information that would usually come later.

Many words or phrases can be moved to the start of a sentence or clause, often followed by a comma:

- Billy cried for two hours.
    → For two hours, Billy cried.
- She played the game cleverly.
    → Cleverly, she played the game.

Information is typically moved to the front of a sentence or clause to ensure an idea is established before the subject or action is shown. As well as being useful for creative scene-setting, this can be important when we want to avoid confusion. Leading with where, when or how an action takes place establishes boundaries for subsequent information, for example. The impact this has depends on the details you move, as is covered below.

5.1.1 Describing Actions

Putting adverbs and adverbial phrases at the front of clauses can affect the way activities and actions are presented. This sort of framing is useful in descriptive language, such as in writing narratives. It is also common in instructions and explanations, where adverbs in the front position add emphasis to manner, focusing on **how** something should be done:

- Thoroughly check the accounts.
- Carefully replace the cap.

It can also affect the pace of your writing:

- She hurriedly locked the door.
- Hurriedly, she locked the door.

Moving the adverb, *hurriedly*, has two effects here. First, we focus on the hurrying, emphasising the nature of her action by leading with it. Second, by placing the describing adverb first, setting up the scene, the action moves quicker afterwards. In this example, the second version has a punchier stop-start, drawing attention to the sudden completion of the action, while the first example flows more neutrally. Neither is better or worse, necessarily; it depends on how it fits into the wider context of a piece of writing. Likewise, the impact of moving *hurriedly* is specific to this example. With a different sentence, and a different adverb, a different result is possible:

- He lazily picked up the chocolate.
- Lazily, he picked up the chocolate.

Using the same technique, moving the adverb forward, the contrast is the same: the first example flows, while the second sets up a scene and completes it. However, while the example with *hurriedly* at the front became punchier, in the example with *lazily* at the front the action slows down.

The reason for this goes back to our first point. Leading with a particular describing word emphasises that describing word, framing the sentence so the writing follows from that idea. The result is one hurried sentence and one lazy sentence, even though they use the same basic structure.

A similar effect can be created by leading a sentence with an action. A **verbal phrase**, the **-ing** form of a verb, or a **phrase that describes an action** can all be used to describe manner:

- Hurrying, she locked the door. *(-ing form of verb)*
- In a hurry, she locked the door. *(prepositional phrase)*

With these examples, the emphasis on *hurry* and its impact on the sentence is similar, so the choice may be a matter of style. However, the prepositional phrase *in a hurry* gives more words to the idea, so the reader may spend more time picturing it. This impacts the pace of the sentence: rather than giving us a stop-start, it stretches out the idea. With the word *hurry* this may make little impact on the reader, but a stronger word, like *panic*, could have more effect:

- Panicking, she locked the door.
- In a panic, she locked the door.

The idea of being *in a panic* creates an image accompanying the locking of the door. With this more specific wording, the reader is not just observing the actions of the character, but can share in her emotional state.

Moving and adapting describing words can therefore produce particular effects depending on an understanding of words' nuances. For more ideas on such considerations, see **8.2 Positioning Describing Words**.

5.1.2 Prepositional Phrases

Moving a prepositional phrase to the front of a clause usually has the impact of setting a scene or presenting an idea before we discuss the action. As prepositional phrases connect nouns, this usually concerns **where** something is done, **with what** it is done, or **within what context**. The reasons for emphasising these details can be varied, though in general this draws attention to additional details surrounding the subject or action:

- In the office, there are 15 desks. *(defining the location)*
- On the grass before the clock tower, we discussed poetry. *(setting the scene)*
- With his wrench, Brandon fixed the pipe. *(creating awareness of the tool first)*
- Amongst Medieval European rulers, Charlemagne stands out as an exceptional leader. *(defining a frame of reference for discussion)*

5.1.3 Time

Placing the time at the start of a clause clearly establishes **when** an event takes place. This is useful when the timing of an action is especially important, or when you want to establish a particular time before describing the action:

- In the evenings, I take my food on the veranda. *(contrasting the idea with other times of day)*
- At three thirty, the bells started ringing. *(emphasising the exact time the event happened)*

- During the rainstorm, they lost sight of the lighthouse. *(setting the scene within a context)*
- In Ancient Times, people settled arguments with stones. *(framing the statement within a particular time period)*

5.2 Rearranging Clauses

Clauses can often be swapped when the order of actions being done is not important, or when you have a dependent clause that defines an object or provides a framing action. As with placing different phrases at the start of the sentence, placing one clause before another emphasises the information that comes first. This can be used to manage the order that we learn something, or to frame an idea before describing the main action. In the following examples, the clauses have been reversed from the usual structure, and the leading clause introduces the action, event, or information:

- Coming down the stairs, Ange noticed a stain on the wall.
- Never taking his eyes off the door, Greg ate his burger.
- In accordance with the rules laid out in subsection 2.1, only copper wiring will be installed.
- While riding the bus through Berlin, Liz studied her guidebook.
- I would have bought that motorboat, if I'd won the jackpot.

The final example is a conditional sentence. When we discuss the condition first, we focus the reader on the imagined situation. By contrast, when we discuss the result first (the **if clause**), we draw attention to the condition required:

- If I raise enough money, I will fly to the moon. *(focusing on the activity needed to satisfy the condition)*
- I will fly to the moon, if I raise enough money. *(focusing on the aspirational result)*

5.3 Parenthetical Information

Additional information can be included almost anywhere in a sentence if we use punctuation to separate text from the main sentence. Exactly how this is done is flexible. It can be with (*brackets*), two dashes – *like this* – or two commas.

Parenthetical information can be a single word, a phrase, a clause, or more. If we remove parenthetical information, the sentence should still make sense. Here are some examples:

- The cows (which are stubborn beasts) could not be persuaded to move. *(a non-defining relative clause, shown with brackets)*
- Your assignment is due no later – and I mean no later – than noon. *(an emphatic additional comment, shown with hyphens)*
- The police searched, half-heartedly, for the missing walrus. *(an extra bit of description, shown with commas)*

In all the above examples, the sentences make complete sense with the parenthetical information removed.

Parenthetical information typically comes directly alongside the idea it relates to. It is useful to add dramatic, emphatic, or informative remarks in unconventional places in a sentence:

- The dungeon, dripping with goo and smelling like an unwashed horse's tail, was not a pleasant place to sleep. *(The subject sets the scene; we add dramatic detail, before commenting on the entire experience.)*
- The trains will – we have been promised – be running on time. *(This remark interrupts a verb phrase, emphasising an attitude towards the word **will**.)*
- Stir the cake mix vigorously until smooth (when the lumps are gone, you're done), then pour it into the pan. *(An extra point of reference is offered for the adverbial **until smooth**.)*

Adding such parenthetical information works in moderation because it creates a break from the normal and expected structure of a sentence. It should be done rarely, however, as overuse will lead to writing that does not flow well.

6. Paragraphs

Paragraphs are used to separate ideas in writing. They are crucial for structuring any writing longer than a few sentences. Paragraphs are typically taught to be between three and five sentences long, with an introductory sentence followed by supporting sentences. Both paragraph length and structure, however, may depend on your personal needs and preferences.

6.1 Paragraph Length

Though typical paragraphs do include similar numbers of sentences, in extreme cases they may be as short as a single sentence or as long as dozens of sentences. Different fields of writing follow different conventions for paragraphs, setting different expectations. You would not typically include unusually short paragraphs in essays, for example. Short, snappy paragraphs are common in journalism and modern novels, however, and screenwriting, in particular, places an emphasis on very short blocks of text.

In general, using the suggested three to five sentences as a target for a paragraph is a good way to focus your writing (similar to setting word limits). Paragraphs of this length create frequent breaks, both for the eye and for ideas, which make it easier for a reader to follow. This is not a hard rule, but it ensures paragraphs contain a good amount of detail without being overlong.

Longer paragraphs may be used when a single idea needs to be discussed in a continuous manner. This is mostly seen in denser academic or other non-fiction texts. In creative writing, such paragraphs are found more in classical literature than modern works. It is rare that such a use is really necessary.

Short, sharp paragraphs can help break up otherwise dense text with a simple, clear idea. This technique can be used to express an exclamation or a sudden, surprising piece of information. In non-fiction, a stand-alone sentence can introduce or conclude an idea emphatically, or it can frame or label other information (such as around graphs and tables). Short paragraphs are also necessary for dialogue, which typically uses a new paragraph for each speaker. The following example shows how a short paragraph can be used for dramatic effect, with a self-contained, surprising detail:

> Hank and Kylie had spent hours climbing the hill to get to the house, and now they were finally there. The view was perfect, with the sun going down and the mountains rising above them in the distance. It looked warm inside, and they'd been promised a welcome meal, so the couple raced the final distance to the door. Hank bumped his shoulder against the door as he tried to turn the handle. He looked at Kylie in shock.

> It was locked.

Such techniques should be used sparingly. Typical paragraph lengths work best for the most part, without drawing attention to your structure, while longer or shorter paragraphs can be used thoughtfully and infrequently to add impact to a particular idea. Repeated use of such variations weakens the effect: too many short paragraphs can lead to snappy, abrupt text, while too many long paragraphs can become difficult to follow and tiring to read.

6.2 Paragraph Structure

The order of information within a paragraph can be rearranged to produce different effects. Early information is typically thought to present the **main idea** of a paragraph, often framing the following information. As with the theory of structure that appears elsewhere in English, we introduce an idea, we explore it, we complete it:

> The party was fantastic. There were dozens of people there, in beautifully colourful clothing. They were drinking and dancing and talking, and everyone seemed to be having a good time. Harriet had been enjoying herself thoroughly, in fact, until Mario arrived.

This example paragraph introduces the overall concept (it was an enjoyable party), followed by elaborating details, and concludes with a twist that challenges the enjoyment of the party (bridging us to the next idea). A natural break comes at the end of this example, as to continue would be to shift to a new idea, such as the impact of Mario's arrival on the party or a discussion of Harriet's problem with him. This same principle can be applied to other fields of writing; for example, in a non-fiction report:

> The new trains were a great success, even though they cost a lot of money to implement. They held more passengers and ran faster than the trains they replaced, and surveys said they were much more aesthetically pleasing. The degree of their success, in fact, suggests it would be wise to order more trains at the earliest convenience.

Again, we have an overall idea with elaborating details and a concluding statement that would require a new idea to follow.

These examples both use fairly typical paragraph structures. As well as illustrating overall structure, they are good indicators of typical length and the order of ideas. Both list and build up details in groups or no more than three, which is a common practice. Lists of three ideas or details give variety without becoming too long, and the **one-two-three** pattern has an agreeable rhythm. These examples also follow a logical, linear order.

When writing a paragraph that covers contrasting information – for example, weighing up the positives and negatives of a single point of an argument – look for logical ways to group that information. In this example, the paragraph discusses the pros and cons of cycling, with the pros and the cons grouped together:

> The benefits of cycling include exercising your body and travelling to places, fast. You can go further on a bike than you can when running, so you can see new things and feel like you've achieved more. Cycling is also a technical sport that makes owning a bike and its equipment a fun hobby. However, cycling does not exercise your whole body, and puts a particular strain on your knees. It is also expensive to buy a bike, and you need somewhere to store it.

There are no specific rules as to how this is done, and deciding which group of ideas you lead with (for example, positives followed by negatives) can depend on your specific stance and style. The main point, though, is that you consider how these different ideas connect within the structure of your paragraph.

As with restructuring sentences, you may reverse the order of a paragraph to add emphasis, or to create a different flow. An idea can be emphasised at the start of a paragraph, but you may also add emphasis at the end; for instance, when revealing a surprising or extreme detail:

> The light was off and the moon couldn't penetrate the grimy windows. Odd noises were coming from the corner: there was a gargling sound like a blocked sink. The shapes before him stuck out from the shadows like clawing fingers. He should not have entered the cellar.

In this example, the final sentence gives an overall comment on the character's location and his decision to go there. We could describe the character and his situation first, but by putting the atmospheric details before the character, we add more drama and entice the reader.

Reversing the order of the usual paragraph structure can also affect how information is interpreted, such as for character development in this example:

> Uncle Greg was a lot of fun, and always had a range of party games to entertain the children. He could be charming when he wanted to, and delighted the ladies with his stories. Uncle Greg was also a terrible drunk, though, and rarely paid for his share of the bill.

Here, the information we close with gives the final, and therefore strongest, impression of Uncle Greg. If we reversed the details and finished with Uncle Greg's positive qualities, it would sound more forgiving of the negatives.

Such techniques can be applied in all areas of writing, and can just as well be used to help emphasise your conclusions in an essay:

> The new system of government brought order and improved the economy. Industry was stimulated by the renewed investments in manufacturing, and crime levels were brought to an all-time low. However, the ruler was an unaccountable tyrant, and far too many people died.

6.3 Formatting Paragraphs

Paragraphs are usually divided in one of two ways: starting on a new line with an indent, or separated from another paragraph by a blank line. Paragraphs separated by a blank line are not usually indented as well.

The format you use for separating paragraphs depends on the style of your writing, so be wary of the conventions used in your particular situation. Emails and printed letters, for example, usually favour a line-break for paragraphs rather than an indent, while a manuscript for publication (such as this book) usually requires indents rather than line-breaks, with blank lines often being used to indicate section breaks.

6.4 Connecting Paragraphs

With longer texts, it can be tempting to connect paragraphs and ideas with bridging words and phrases such as *therefore, thus, then, in addition*, etc. In most cases, such words actually reduce flow by making your language more complicated without adding detail. If your paragraphs break at logical points, the next idea should flow naturally without using such indicators.

Watch out for bridging words and phrases and remove them whenever you can. This will simplify your text and help you test whether or not your paragraphs follow logically. It will also make such bridging words more effective when they are actually needed.

7. Vocabulary

Widening your vocabulary is essential to improve in any language skill. The more words you know, the more subjects you can discuss with greater accuracy. Advanced vocabulary helps you to be more specific. Wider understanding of words helps you to read more and to understand people from different regions or cultures. However, the more words you learn, the more caution you need when using them.

A wide vocabulary can harm your writing if you use words inappropriately or inaccurately. This may happen when you use a word your reader does not understand or if you use a word outside its correct context. It can also happen when you use language that is more complex than is necessary, negatively affecting the reading experience. Your writing's main job is to communicate effectively, and difficult or uncommon vocabulary can prevent that.

7.1 Using Advanced Words

Consider the following two sentences:

- Arthur sat on a wooden bench and quietly drank some milk.
- Arthur parked his rear on a timber bench and tacitly consumed a pasteurised beverage.

The second sentence might seem impressive if you want to demonstrate how many different words you know, but it does not create a clear picture. It does not communicate its main idea effectively.

Using advanced vocabulary requires two levels of understanding. First, you must learn the word's meaning. Second, you must learn when it should be used. Properly understood, advanced vocabulary should be applied strategically for a particular effect.

Considering our example again, we could use one advanced word at a time, for different purposes:

- Arthur sat on a wooden bench and **tacitly** drank some milk. *(emphasising his shyness with an advanced word that may also hint at his intelligence)*
- Arthur sat on a wooden bench and quietly drank some **pasteurised** milk. *(focusing on the technical aspect of the drink, perhaps demonstrating a health-conscious character, or a detail-focused writer)*

The notes in brackets may seem like an extreme interpretation, but this is the level of consideration that makes your use of advanced vocabulary effective. Your particular purpose is likely to depend on the wider context. In the form of a narrative, such considerations may be used to reflect the personality of the central character:

- Arthur, a scientist who spent more time with books than people, perched on the bench and sipped what he considered to be a very tasty beverage.

This sentence conveys more than the idea of our simple scene. Here, we are communicating Arthur's personality through a pompous narrative style. What if we wanted to give him a different tone?

- Arthur plonked himself on the bench and downed his milk.

This example takes a jump from advanced vocabulary to informal, regional vocabulary. Such a vocabulary choice has a big impact on tone.

In non-fiction writing, reflecting such attitudes and tones is far less common, making it safer to stick to simpler vocabulary choices. However, advanced vocabulary is common when specific vocabulary is necessary or expected, and certain subjects require specialist language for discussion. Academic, medical, and business terms, for example, often represent ideas which do not have a simpler alternative; words which should be commonly understood when read by a like-minded audience. This is discussed in more detail in the next section, **7.2 Specialist Vocabulary**.

As a guiding rule, keep in mind the concept of **simplicity**. Choose the most common word, or (generally) the shorter word, unless you have a good reason not to. Deciding on a good reason for using advanced vocabulary is where your personal understanding of language becomes very important. Essentially, the only reason for using advanced vocabulary is that the specific function of a word is necessary to convey a specific point. If not, choose the word most likely to be understood.

It is likely that the first words you learnt in English will be the words you continue to use most. And that's a good thing.

7.2 Specialist Vocabulary

Even when you wish to keep your writing simple, specialist vocabulary may be necessary to discuss specific subject matters. This is important when dealing with subjects with unique identifying words (such as medical terms) or concepts (such as mathematical terms). It also occurs in creative writing when you wish to create a very specific image. Consider the following example, which uses advanced vocabulary to discuss a medical condition:

> Fibromyalgia is a condition that causes pain across the body. It can lead to a number of symptoms, including increased sensitivity to pain, muscle stiffness, and fatigue.

Notice that although this short paragraph uses a number of advanced words, it also uses very simple words. If you don't know what *fibromyalgia* is, the simple language helps introduce it. Though it is an advanced concept, no more advanced language is necessary around it, and other advanced words would only make it confusing (consider: *Fibromyalgia is chronic disorder capable of causing multiple symptoms, including heightened sensitivity...*). The specialist words are used when needed to cover specifics: *fatigue*, for example, is more appropriate than the simpler *tiredness* as it suggests a chronic medical condition rather than ordinary tiredness.

Exactly when do you need specialist words, then? They may be necessary for a subject with no simple alternative (such as *fibromyalgia*). Advanced vocabulary use may also depend on your audience.

Ask yourself these questions to decide whether or not to use an advanced word:

1. Who will read your text?
2. Will your reader understand this word?
3. Is this word necessary?

Your use of advanced language may change depending on who you are writing for. An article in a medical journal may use very different vocabulary to an article on the same topic in a health magazine. Our example above may indeed use *tiredness* over *fatigue* for publication in a high street magazine.

The best way to understand what level of specialist vocabulary is appropriate for your reader is to read widely in your field. What sort of language do others use? Is their meaning clear?

For further examples, study the range of English language newspapers available. In the UK, the vocabulary used in *The Times* is of a much higher level than that used in the tabloids. This does not necessarily make the language better or worse, it is simply written with a particular audience in mind. A reader of *The Times* may be someone with an expanded vocabulary, while tabloids are read by people who want something light and easy.

After studying how others write, you must also make your own judgements for the correct balance of vocabulary. Beware that others are not necessarily following the principles of being clear and simple with their language. Unnecessary advanced vocabulary is particularly common in areas such as business writing, where specialist language may be negatively labelled with terms like **management speak** or **office jargon**. Many popular terms in business, particularly in management, are used because they are fashionable (buzzwords), but don't add meaning. Such language can cause resentment when readers think it is being used for the wrong reasons. Examples include clichéd idioms, such as *think outside the box* or *square the circle*, or 'new' words or phrases which have an adequate existing English expression, such as *actionable* instead of *task*. This can complicate simple ideas, rather than providing labels for otherwise undefined ideas. Always keep this in mind when reading the work of other writers: observe when and why advanced language is used, and consider for yourself what is acceptable and effective.

7.3 Synonyms

The English language has been adapted over many centuries to include words from various European (and other) languages, and therefore contains a great number of words and phrases which can be used interchangeably, or with similar effect. Using advanced vocabulary in the place of more common words can add variety and flow to your writing. However, remember that the most obvious or simplest choice of words is often the clearest, and using an alternative requires a good reason.

You are likely to use a synonym for one of two reasons:

1. The synonym is more specific/appropriate *(for example, because of a subtle difference in meaning)*.
2. Your style requires a different word *(for example, to help the sentence flow or to create an appropriate tone)*.

Note that avoiding repetition is not necessarily a good style choice on its own. When we avoid repetition, it is to help with the flow or tone of the writing, and you should not avoid repetition of words for its own sake. This is discussed in full detail in the next section, **7.4 Avoiding Repetition**.

Choosing appropriate synonyms depends on your understanding of words in context. Sometimes, synonyms can be used interchangeably with no difference in meaning, but in a different context, a subtle difference emerges:

*   Marian proved herself strong/tough enough to stand up to the bullies. *(**Strong/tough** both refer, generally, to her character.)*
*   Marian won the weight-lifting contest because she was strong. *(**Strong** refers to physical strength, answering **how much** she could lift.)*
*   Marian won the weight-lifting contest because she was tough. *(**Tough** refers more to endurance – physical or mental.)*

Such differences are not always noticeable or important, but even words that almost always mean the same thing may sometimes be interpreted differently. The differences can be very nuanced, though some patterns can be seen in formal and informal vocabulary.

English combines Anglo Saxon and Old French vocabularies (among others). In general, words of French origin tend to be longer and have more varied spelling rules than Anglo Saxon words, which are often short and simple. A hierarchy exists between these synonyms, partly due to Old French being introduced as a stately/superior language during the Middle Ages. In part, perhaps, it is also due to longer/difficult words sounding more educated. For example *chauffeur*, a word of French origin, is used to make a *driver* sound more important. Likewise we can *buy* something, or we can *purchase* it, with the only difference being how polite or formal you want the word to sound. These subtle differences can change the tone of your writing, even when using words that mean the same thing.

The following table compares some of the Anglo Saxon and Old French synonyms, to help make you aware of the options.

Anglo Saxon	Old French
almighty	omnipotent
amaze / stun	astound
anger / wrath	ire
answer	reply / response
ask	enquire
awesome	incredible
bear	carry
behaviour	manner
belief	faith
belongings	property
brittle	frail / fragile
buy	purchase
daring / boldness	audacity
darling	favourite
deal	amount
dearth	famine
deem	consider / judge
drink	beverage
fair / fair-haired	blond(e)
fall / harvest	autumn
foe	enemy
folk	people
follow	ensue

Anglo Saxon	Old French
forgive	pardon
freedom	liberty
friendly	amicable
ghost	phantom
grave	tomb
graveyard	cemetery
harbour	port
hearty	cordial
help	aid / assist
hunt	chase
inn	tavern
lawyer	attorney
leave	permission
lovely	beautiful
ruthless	remorseless
sake	reason / cause
selfhood	identity
shirt	blouse
smell	odour
span	distance
stern	severe
thorough	exhaustive
tough	difficult
tumble	somersault
unwilling / loath	reluctant
uphold	support
weak	feeble / faint
weapon	arm
weep / sob	cry
weird	strange
wholesome	salubrious
wild	savage
wilful	deliberate
wisdom	prudence / sagacity
wish / will	desire
wonder	ponder
woodland	forest
woodwork	carpentry
worthy	valuable

Though this reflects a general truth, not all words of Old French origin are considered more advanced or formal than the Anglo Saxon equivalent. In some cases there is little or no difference in formality, and in a few rare cases the Anglo Saxon word may now be used more formally, usually because the Old French version has become adopted so commonly that the less common Anglo Saxon version stands out. For example, *hue* (of Anglo Saxon origin) sounds more technical than the more generally adopted *colour*. Likewise *uncouth* (of Anglo Saxon origin) is used more formally than *rude* (Old French), because it is now less common.

With certain synonyms, different words have also developed more exclusive meanings through use. This is particularly clear in the case of foods, where the Old French words for animals refer to food types while the Anglo Saxon names are used for the animals themselves.

Anglo Saxon	Old French
chicken	poultry
cow	beef
deer	venison
pig	pork
sheep	mutton

Knowing this would be crucially important when writing a restaurant menu, or any food-related text. Similar differences may occur in other specialist areas, depending on the context you are writing in.

Synonyms are also not always transferable: in sports, you might have a *referee* or *umpire* depending on the sport (e.g. referee in football, umpire in tennis). Keep this in mind as you expand your vocabulary. It is not enough to know that one word or phrase has the same meaning as another, you need to ask when it is appropriate (or not) to use each variation.

7.4 Avoiding Repetition

A common writing tip is to avoid repetition for more effective writing. This may be given as a rule, such as to avoid using the same word twice in a sentence, or in a paragraph. This tip is useful to create better flow and more accurate language use in your writing. It can be applied with synonyms for all word types and even when looking at repeated phrases.

A starting point is to avoid the repetition of nouns by using pronouns:

- The lake was cold. The lake was always cold in the winter.
  → The lake was cold. It was always cold in the winter.

For describing words, repetition may highlight the need to either simplify your writing or to think of more accurate details. Both solutions can create a clearer and more engaging image for the reader:

- His goal in life was to own a big house with many rooms and a big garden.
  → His goal in life was to own a four-bed house with a spacious garden.

Repeated verbs can slow down your text, making your writing seem dull and uninteresting. You can avoid repeating verbs by grouping clauses together for a smoother reading experience:

- Mary wanted to go to the cinema. She wanted to see a romance film, and wanted to get some popcorn.
  → Mary wanted to go to the cinema, see a romance film, and get some popcorn.

As with describing words, looking out for repetition of verbs can also be a cue to look for more accurate verbs. In this example, *wanted* could be replaced by *longed* to add more emotion:

- Mary wanted to go to the cinema. She longed to see a romance film and get some popcorn.

Adding variety can create additional considerations, though. With the structure of this example, we group both the film *and* the popcorn under the more characterful *longing*. Perhaps Mary does *long* to do both activities, but if you change a verb, you must consider the whole sentence.

In this case, if her emotion regarding the popcorn is heightened it may be more appropriate that Mary *longs* to *eat* the popcorn rather than simply *get* it:

- Mary wanted to go to the cinema. She longed to see a romance film and eat some popcorn.

Next, note that we are not avoiding repetition by simply adding variety. These changes help the sentence flow better. Simply adding variety, without considering the impact, could be worse than using repetition:

- Mary pined to go to the cinema. She coveted to see a romance film and lusted to buy some popcorn.

As well as creating a more confusing sentence for the reader, this example creates grammatical problems, as not all verbs behave the same way (we should covet *something*, and lust *for* or *after*).

The examples here are brief, for the purposes of illustrating the point. In longer texts, with wider contexts, you may have more specific and detailed reasons for choosing to include or to avoid repetition. Consider the difference even a single word can make to the appropriateness of this repetition, though:

- Spoilt Mary wanted to go to the cinema. She wanted to see a romance film and she wanted to get popcorn.

Now the repeated verb works alongside the character-trait of Mary being spoilt, to put a clear and appropriate emphasis on how obnoxious Mary is. Repetition can be used in this way to add emphasis. It could also be used deliberately to stress Mary's series of desires, or to emphasise how much she wants it. Repeating the same noun can highlight a specific subject and repeating an action can demonstrate special attention or annoyance from that activity. How and why we apply repetition in this way is further covered in **14.4 Repetition for Emphasis**.

Creating variety in your language is therefore rarely as simple as avoiding repetition as a rule. No one can tell you how soon is too soon to repeat a word, phrase or idea. It depends on your text. Some would say, for example, never to repeat a particularly advanced word within one text, but if your text is incredibly long, or one where that word is frequently relevant, then such a rule makes no sense. By all means look out for repeated words, phrases, and ideas in your text, but do not tell yourself they must be changed. Instead, ask yourself if they are the best way to convey your meaning.

Sometimes a repeated word is simply the most clear and/or most appropriate word to use. Your writing can become confusing if you add unnatural vocabulary to avoid repetition.

How do you know, then, if your repeated language needs changing or not? Start by asking if it is necessary to repeat the word or phrase at all. Brevity helps focus your writing, and removing repetition encourages simpler writing:

- There were squirrels on the lawn, digging holes in the lawn and hiding nuts.
  →There were squirrels on the lawn, digging holes and hiding nuts.

Next, consider if the repeated word or phrase is the most effective way to convey your idea. Bear in mind that the best word is not always the simplest or the most specific, and it is not always a word that is different. It is often just the word that will be **most easily understood**. In these examples, the first is simplest but its meaning is unclear, the second is the most specific but it sounds clumsy, and the third, with repetition, is easiest to read:

- The squirrels turned viciously towards the children. They ran. *(Does **they** refer to the squirrels or the children?)*
- The squirrels turned viciously towards the children. The group of young people ran. / The boys and girls ran. *(These versions are cumbersome, slowing the pace.)*
- The squirrels turned viciously towards the children. The children ran.

7.5 Regional Variations

English is used so widely that vocabulary understood in one region is not necessarily known in another. Sometimes, regional differences are commonly understood, or at least easily noticeable, such as variations in British English and American English (e.g. *underground* vs *subway*, *trousers* vs *pants*). Other regional differences stretch beyond vocabulary, such as naming conventions, how to format times and dates, and certain grammar rules (such as whether an adverb sounds natural before or after an auxiliary verb). How can you ensure, then, that your writing will be understood if it is to be read by someone from a different region?

The best advice is to be accurate and consistent within your own regional understanding of English. It is perfectly acceptable to use regional language and styles as long as you are consistent (and as long as you can recognise when a regional difference has caused, or has the potential to cause, confusion). Use spelling, vocabulary and grammar that is consistent to one region. Do not mix regional spellings. When your writing will be read in a different region, avoid highly regionally specific language such as local terms and phrases.

You can develop your own understanding by always paying attention to regional differences in your reading. When writing for a specific region, read widely from their literature to develop an idea of their vocabulary. When you perceive repeated mistakes in spelling or grammar in different texts, ask yourself if they share a regional variation. This is particularly important when dealing with idiomatic words and phrases.

If you are specifically writing for people in a different region, or for a general readership, it can be sensible to highlight the specific language you have chosen to write in. For example, when a text in British English may be read by an American, such as with this book, you can make a note of it as I have in the introduction:

> Please note that this book is written in British English and follows UK style conventions, though it is intended for readers all over the world. Although consideration has been given to the differences between British and American English, it may contain regionally specific language.

8. Descriptions and Details

Adjectives and adverbs add flavour to writing, and can transform flat description into something clearer, more detailed, and more dynamic. Such effects require careful use, however; poorly chosen describing words can be confusing, while badly placed describing words interrupt flow.

8.1 Using Describing Words Carefully

Many professional writers have highlighted the importance of limiting your describing words as a step towards better writing. Advice against the over-use of adjectives and adverbs essentially focuses on two principles.

8.1.1 Beware Decorative Describing Words

Writers often add describing words to make a sentence more interesting, but the chosen word adds little detail. Such decorative describing words are either irrelevant or inappropriate. They usually occur when you have an adjective or adverb that is made redundant by other words in your sentence:

- a big lorry *(most lorries are big)*
- He quickly ran for the bus. *(It is obvious he would run quickly.)*
- It was a grim and miserable day. *(two very similar adjectives)*

Decorative describing words are particularly noticeable when a writer wants to demonstrate an advanced vocabulary:

- The cola bubbled effervescently. *(The adverb **effervescently** is overly elaborate and, while interesting, tells us nothing more than **bubbled**.)*

8.1.2   Use Effective Nouns and Verbs Before Describing Words

The best way to remove a describing word is to use a more specific noun or verb. In the examples above, *big lorry* and *quickly ran* are examples where the noun or verb goes some way towards making the describing word unnecessary. Replace *quickly ran* with *sprinted* and the adverb is no longer any use. Readers can usually fill in details themselves, if you give them the right clues. Consider the different reading experience in the following examples, where better noun and verb choices remove the need for describing words:

- He put his feet up on the short, stumpy object before the sofa.
  → He put his feet up on the footstool.
- "Get over here!" she shouted loudly and forcibly.
  → "Get over here!" she commanded.

As well as applying to adjectives and adverbs, the principles of avoiding decorative language and choosing more appropriate nouns and verbs can apply more generally to the details you include in your writing. With the correct signposts, a reader only needs a few words to create an entire image. You do not need to describe a market as *bustling*, *full of people*, or *crowded*, for example, when *busy market* conjures the image well enough for most people. This applies in both fiction and non-fiction writing. It is not necessary to spell out every detail of a project or academic concept if you know your audience is familiar with the details. With the correct word (if your reader will know what it means), a lot of detail can be removed:

- a wooden ship with sails → a galleon
- a small, luxurious ship with a sail → a yacht
- a long, heavy ship holding many large containers
  → a cargo ship

Being efficient in this way makes writing simpler and clearer, so it is quicker to read and better engages the reader. It also gives readers an opportunity to picture things through their own imaginative lens, which is why readers often enjoy books more than their film counterparts.

With all this in mind, how do you actually use describing words?

Adjectives and adverbs serve a very useful purpose. You just need to know the difference between a **decorative** describing word and an **effective** one. A decorative describing word adds little or no information, while an effective one adds depth to your writing. Consider this description and ask yourself which describing words are useful:

> The suit he wore was grey and closely hugged his body; it was made from expensive, carefully chosen material, tightly stitched without a thread out of place, all the same slate colour with a small, intricate logo woven into the lapel.

When you decide what the most important details are, and you strip out the decorative words, the remaining text is more effective:

> His slate suit was tightly stitched, with an intricate logo woven into the lapel.

Focusing on only the *tight stitching* and *intricate logo* implies other details. A tightly stitched suit should fit well and is typically expensive, and with the shorter description, the distinctive logo now stands out more.

To do this takes practice, but if you pay attention to how your descriptions are constructed it will help develop your vocabulary and sense for the most important details. Do as much as you can with as few words as possible. Start with the noun and verb before moving onto adjectives and adverbs, and you'll find it easier to use describing words.

8.2 Positioning Describing Words

The position of your descriptions can have a big impact on your writing. While other words may have a clear place in a sentence (the positions of nouns, verbs, and determiners are rarely very flexible), describing words move around more freely. This offers opportunities for both creativity and mistakes, however.

When in doubt, stick to the basics; place adjectives and adverbs directly before the word they modify.

Adjectives can also be placed after a noun, pronoun, or verb when they provide detail for a verb that modifies the noun:

- He is tall.
- This text became complicated.

Adverbs, meanwhile, are used in many different locations depending on their function; adverbs of manner, time, and frequency, for example, all behave differently. Adverb positions can also be nuanced and regional. There is not always a right or wrong position for an adverb, or adverbial phrase, so pay close attention to how others use them. (For more details on how adverbs fit into sentences, see my book *Word Order in English Sentences*.)

When using more than one describing word, order the list with care. Native English speakers stick to a natural pattern. Describing words are usually listed from **general to specific**, and **opinion comes before fact**.

- the weird, big brown tree
- our mad, violent, and penniless elder brother

In the examples above, reversing the orders would seem unnatural and change the emphasis of the phrase. Changes could also impact the overall meaning: *our elder mad, violent, and penniless brother*, for example, implies you are the discussing the older of two or more brothers who are mad, violent, and penniless. It may not always be interpreted this way, but if there is a possibility of creating confusion it should be avoided.

Multiple adjectives before a noun can be presented as a list, separated by commas. A conjunction (e.g. *and*) is usually not needed when the adjectives are before the noun, but you do need *and* when the list comes after the noun:

- We have a small, square, beige car.
- Our car is small, square, and beige.

You can use *and* for a list of adjectives before a noun to change the word order and put emphasis on the final adjective (which is useful for opinion adjectives). Consider:

- They entered a dark, dreary and frankly disgusting sewer.

As with general structure, if your list includes varying viewpoints, it's usually best to group describing words logically (such as positives before negatives):

- My car was fast and comfortable, but cheap. *(NOT My car was fast but cheap, and also comfortable.)*

The **Rule of Three** works well with listing adjectives. Three describing words add variety and an agreeable rhythm, but more than three adjectives can make the sentence clumsy. Keep in mind, though, that more effective description typically means limiting your describing words. This is particularly true of adverbs. If you are in a situation where you need to use more than one adverb, consider revising your sentence, as there is probably a better way to make your point. For example, *he cheerily, energetically, and smilingly cooked the pasta* sounds clumsy. There are many ways to improve it, but one would be to replace the adverbs with one more appropriate word: *he joyously cooked the pasta* (*cheerily* could also work on its own here).

Exceptions to these ideas occur when we want to add emphasis or present surprising information. Describing words can be placed in different orders within a list, or in different places within a sentence. One way to do this is with parenthetical information, or dependent descriptive clauses, which can come after a noun or after a crucial piece of information:

- He shook the man's hand, wet and clammy, and cringed.

This parenthetical description comes at the time that the character feels the hand, so we have the image of him shaking before the sensation.

- The speech was well-received, short and encouraging as it was.

This dependent clause places the description afterwards, as secondary information, so we learn the response *(well-received)* before considering the speech's qualities *(short and encouraging)*.

- Smelly and vaguely green, the cheese had clearly gone bad.

This sentence leads with a description, drawing immediate attention to these details for maximum impact before we know what is being described.

9. Spelling

English is not a phonetic language, so words are not always spelt as they sound. There are twenty vowel sounds but only eight vowels in the alphabet. Other variations come from words adopted from different languages.

Many English spelling rules are taught, but these often have so many exceptions they are difficult to apply. For example, a popular mnemonic rhyme in English schools is: **I before E except after C**. This helps with choosing between *ie* or *ei* when spelling words like *friends, believe* and *receive*. However, it does not apply to many common words, such as *their, weird,* and *neighbour*. Nevertheless, inaccurate spelling can completely change the meaning of your writing, and such patterns are a necessary starting point to avoid mistakes.

You can find plenty of lists of spelling rules online, for instance on the Cambridge Dictionary webpage listed in the **Recommended Reading** section. It is also a good idea to have a respected dictionary like the *New Oxford Dictionary* on hand when writing.

This chapter covers some of the rules which all writers should know.

9.1 General Spelling Rules

9.1.1 Plurals

Plurals are typically created by adding **-s** to a word:

- cat → cat**s**
- dreadnought → dreadnought**s**

For words ending with a **-ch** or **-s** sound, **-es** is added, making it easier to say:

- church → church**es**
- bus → bus**es**

With words ending in **consonant + y** (e.g -*ly*, -*ny*), replace **-y** with **-ies**:

- party → part**ies**
- company → compan**ies**

With words ending with **vowel + y**, only add **-s**:

- bay → bay**s**
- key → key**s**

With words ending with a short vowel followed by **-f** or **-fe**, usually change **-f** to **-ves**:

- half → hal**ves**
- knife → kni**ves**
- yourself → yoursel**ves**

However, **-f** does not change for plurals of words with a **double f** (e.g. *cliff* → *cliffs*) and with many words that have a long vowel before the -f (e.g. *oaf* → *oafs*, *chief* → *chiefs*, *roof* → *roofs*).

9.1.2 Words ending in E

When adding a suffix that begins with a vowel (e.g. *-ing, -able, -ible*) to words that end in **-e**, the **-e** is usually removed:

- make → making
- cite → citation
- note → notable

This is also true when adding **-ed**, for example for verb forms, as the **-e** should not be doubled (an alternative perspective is to add **-d**, instead of **-ed**):

- rotate → rotat**ed**
- stake → stak**ed**

When adding **-ing** to words ending in -e, the -e- is sometimes still used, to separate similar words with different meanings:

- die → dying *(to expire)*
- dye → dyeing *(to colour)*

The -e is not typically removed for suffixes beginning with a consonant:

- excite → excitement
- whole → wholesome

There are exceptions to this, though:

- whole → wholly
- due → duly

9.1.3 Words Ending in Y

When adding suffixes to words ending **consonant + y**, the -y changes to -i-:

- hurry → hurried
- comply → compliance

The -y does not usually change if the word ends **vowel + y**, with the suffix -**ing**, or when adding **'s**:

- play → play**er**
- reply → reply**ing**
- nanny → nanny**'s** *(though note,* nannies *would be the plural)*

9.1.4 Doubling Consonants

Usually, consonants are doubled when adding a suffix starting with a vowel (e.g. *-ed, -ing, -est*) to a word ending with a single vowel and a single consonant. This is true when creating all word types, whether a noun, adjective, adverb, or verb form. It depends on the consonant (usually *b, d, g, l, m, n, p, r,* and *t*). With words of more than one syllable, the consonant is usually only doubled if the stress is on the last syllable (see overleaf):

- bid → bi**dd**ing
- rid → ri**dd**ance
- pen → pe**nn**ed
- general → genera**ll**y

There are exceptions to these rules though, so be careful with different words (particularly when dealing with words ending in -**er**):

- visit → visiting
- enter → entered

The doubling of consonants is not always easy to guess – especially when the stress in a multi-syllable changes from the stress in the root word:

- *prefer* becomes *prefe**rred*** (stress on *-fer-*) but also *prefe**rence*** (stress on *pre-*)
- *refer* becomes *refe**rred*** (stress on *-fer-*) but also *refe**rence*** (stress on *ref-*)
- BUT *occur* becomes *occu**rred*** (stress on *-cur-*) and *occu**rrence*** (stress on *-cur-*)

9.1.5 Verb Forms

Verbs commonly change forms, with spelling rules for **regular verbs**.

The Present Simple

The present simple is formed by either using the root of a verb on its own, or by adding -**s** (or -**es**) to the root for third person singular subjects *(he, she, it, John, an object)*.

- The cat **walks**. *(+ s because it is third person singular)*
- Cats **walk** silently. *(no -s because it is a plural)*
- I **like** reading. *(no -s because it is first person)*

The Past

For the past tense, and regular past participles, add **-ed** to the root verb:

- to walk → walk**ed**
- to play → play**ed**
- to book → book**ed**

Regular verbs that end with **-e** end in **-ed** (no double e):

- I mov**ed**. *(to move)*
- We settl**ed** the bill. *(to settle)*

The double-consonant rule applies, so verbs may add **consonant + ed**:

- We man**ned** the office. *(to man)*
- He plot**ted** to overthrow the king. *(to plot)*

Similarly, changing the final **-y** to **-i-** and adding **-ed** can also apply to verbs. This happens when there is a consonant before the **-y**:

- She stud**ied**. *(to study)*
- They marr**ied**. *(to marry)*

For some short verbs ending in **vowel + y**, you remove the **-y** and add **-id** instead of **-ied**. These are considered irregular:

- I pa**id** my taxes. *(to pay)*
- He la**id** the table. *(to lay)*

You may see a number of regular verbs that add **-t** instead of **-ed**. Many of these verbs have two past forms. Both the **-t** and **-ed** forms have been considered correct in different times and places. Common examples include *burned / burnt, earned / earnt,* and *learned / learnt*. Various rules try to explain the differences, which are discussed in **9.3 Regional Spelling Variations**. Using (or not using) each is ultimately a matter of style. Beware, though: the pronunciation of many past verbs may sound like they end in **-t**, but only a select few verbs use **-t** as an accepted spelling.

Present Participles

The present participle is formed by using the **stem of the verb** + **-ing**: for instance, *read* → *reading*. The present participle is the same for all subjects:

- I was read**ing**.
- She was read**ing** in the rain.
- They were read**ing** too loud.

Regular **-ing** forms follow word ending rules, for example dropping **-e** or doubling consonants, but **-ing** forms do not usually remove a final **y**:

- to excite → excit**ing**
- to run → run**ning**
- to hurry → hurry**ing**

Irregular Verbs

The above rules are useful when dealing with regular verbs, but there are over 200 irregular verbs in common use in the English language, and many hundreds more in expanded vocabulary. For these, you have to familiarise yourself with individual spellings, as they are difficult to accurately group. Lists of irregular verbs are available on the internet: for an example, see the Wikipedia webpage on the **Recommended Reading** list.

9.1.6 Other Endings

There are many additional ways that words can be changed, particularly when forming other words, with minor rules for different endings.

In some cases there are useful, common patterns: for example, adding the suffix **-ful** (to mean *full of*), with **one l**:

- care → care**ful**
- mind → mind**ful**

When we add **-ly** to a word ending with **-l**, we usually double the **l**:

- careful → carefully
- general → generally

Such additional patterns are incredibly diverse. There are various online lists which give more rules to help explore other spelling patterns. It is questionable how effectively you can learn spellings by simply reading lists, though. The best practice is to be careful with your spelling and make a note of any similarities or peculiarities that you notice.

9.2 Spelling from Sound

While English is not directly phonetic, there are a number of patterns and rules that may help you spell out words (or at least make a reasonable guess) based on how they sound. This mostly relies on an understanding of the different vowel sounds in English. There are a total of 20 different vowel sounds in English, which can be variously categorised by phonetics for pronunciation. For the purposes of spelling rules, it is useful to break these down into **short vowels**, **long vowels**, and **other vowels**, as these groups relate to letters of the alphabet rather than the phonetic chart. In the following tables the sounds are represented by letters from the International Phonetic Alphabet; if you are unfamiliar with these you may find the sounds represented online, and a link is given in the **Recommended Reading** section.

9.2.1 Short Vowels

Short vowel sounds are usually written with a single vowel followed by a single consonant.

Sound	Usually written	Examples
/æ/	a	mat, pat, lap
/ɛ/	e	met, pet, let
/ɪ/	i	bin, pit, lip
/ɒ/	o	rot, pot, lot
/ʌ/	u	fun, sun, luck

Short vowels may be followed by certain consonant clusters like *ck* or *st* and are commonly found with double consonants in longer words, especially in -**ing** forms of verbs and past participles, for example: *common, swimming, running, rotten.*

9.2.2 Long Vowels

Long vowels are longer equivalents of the five short vowel sounds, with completely different sounds. They are the sounds used to name the letters they correspond to, but they can have a wide variety of spellings. A pattern common to the spelling of the long vowels is **the silent e**, discussed in more detail in **9.2.4 The Silent E**.

Sound	Usually written	Examples
a		
/eɪ/	ai, ay, a-*consonant*-e	wait, day, late
e		
/iː/	ee, ea, y, ie, i-*consonant*-e	sheep, meat, dandy, fiend, elite
i		
/aɪ/	i, ig, igh, y, i-*consonant*-e	I, sign, fight, dry, ice
o		
/əʊ/	oa, o-*consonant*-e	boat, note
u		
/juː/	ew, ue, u-*consonant*-e	few, due, cube

9.2.3 Other Vowels

For the sounds of **a** and **e**, additional vowel sounds are created when the vowel is followed by an **r** sound. Sounds relating to **o** are more diverse: as well as a sound followed by an **r** (as in *for*), four other vowel sounds have roots in **o** spellings, as shown in the following table.

Sound	Usually written	Examples
a		
/ɑː/	ar	far, car
/eə/	ai, a-*consonant*-e, e-*consonant*-e	air, care, where
e		
/ɪə/	ee, ea, e-*consonant*-e	steer, near, here
/ɜː/	er, or, ir, ur	her, word, bird, hurt
o		
/uː/	o, oo, ough	do, doom, through
/ɔɪ/	oi, oy	coin, toy
/ɔː/	o, oa, or, oo, o-*consonant*-e	for, oar, worn, door, more
/aʊ/	ou	sound
/ʊ/	oo	look

9.2.4 The Silent E

Many words in English have an unpronounced **e** at the end, which has the effect of giving a vowel a different sound (usually separated from the **-e** by a consonant or consonant cluster):

- mine
- like
- hate

There are exceptions to this, with words ending in **-e** that still have a short vowel sound, or a different long vowel to that typically associated with the letter (for example, using -*ere* like *air*):

- none
- love
- care
- give
- where

9.2.5 The Schwa

The most common vowel sound in English is the **schwa**. This is the sound of an unstressed syllable, a bit like saying *uh*. With multi-syllable words, the unstressed syllables usually create no distinct sound and become the schwa. Native English speakers are likely to pronounce unstressed suffixes, for instance *-tion, -sion,* and *-cian,* the same way: as *sh-n.* Consider how these words might be written based on their sound:

- contention → *c-ntensh-n*
- decision → *d-sish-n*
- patrician → *patrish-n*

We could reasonably write **u** for the schwa sound, but the schwa is not quite the same as the pronunciation of **u** from *fun* or *sun.* In dictionary guides to pronunciation, the schwa sound is represented by the phonetic symbol ə.

While the rules for the various vowels can give you a starting point for choosing the correct spellings from sounding out words, the right vowel for a schwa sound cannot be easily predicted. Do check and ask for another opinion if you need it.

9.2.6 Consonant Rules

Consonant sounds are typically written with more predictable spellings than vowel sounds, though some consonants have dual sounds (often referred to as **hard** and **soft**, or as **voiced** and **unvoiced**). Discussing differences in consonant sounds requires an understanding of how a sound is voiced within the mouth. For example, the difference between pronouncing **v** and **th** can be described as **labiodental** (using the bottom lip and top teeth) and **dental** (using the tip of the tongue and the top teeth).

Such differences may depend heavily on regional accents (for example, with native speakers who pronounce **th** as an **f**), so such an understanding does not necessarily help with spelling. There are a few common consonant sounds and clusters that you can look out for, however. These are the tip of a complex area for sounding out consonant sounds, but if you are familiar with the basic consonant sounds in English, these points should take you most of the way towards accurate spelling:

- **s** sounds may be spelt with **s**, **c**, or **sc**. For example, *simple, circle,* and *science* all start with the same *s* sound.
- **c** is usually made soft (like an **s**) when followed by **e**, **i**, or **y** *(e.g. cement).* Otherwise, **c** is hard like **k** *(e.g. crisp).*

- **z** sounds are sometimes spelt with **s** *(e.g. rise)* – though **not** at the beginning of a root word *(e.g. zoo)*.
- The soft **j** sound may be spelt with **j** *(juice)* or **g** followed by **e**, **i**, or **y** *(e.g. judge, edgy, genetics)*.
- The **sh** sound is usually spelt **sh** at the start of a word, but can also be spelt **ti**, **ci**, and **si** in later syllables. These spellings are usually found in suffixes such as **-tian**, **-tion**, **-cian** and **-sion** *(e.g. politician, exception, patrician, decision)*.

9.3 Regional Spelling Variations

The main regional variations in English spellings come between the British and American spellings of words.

No regional variation is necessarily right or wrong, as long as you are consistent, but including both British and American spellings within one document would be a mistake. Your choice of regional style may also depend on your context. Consider your audience: if you write for an American audience in British English (or vice versa) without making it clear, your readers may think you have made mistakes.

The following sections explore some common differences between British English and American English spellings.

9.3.1 -our / -or

The cluster **-our** in British English is often spelt **-or** in American English.

British English	American English
armour	armor
colour	color
flavour	flavor
honour	honor
labour	labor
neighbour	neighbor
rumour	rumor

There are exceptions to certain words with **-our**, however. For example, the personal pronouns *your, our, ours,* etc. are the same in British English and

American English. It is also worth noting that some words lose the **u** in British English when you add a suffix, for example: *humour* → *humorous*.

9.3.2 -re / -er

Many words ending -**re** in British English are spelt -**er** in American English.

British English	American English
calibre	caliber
centre	center
fibre	fiber
litre	liter
metre	meter
theatre	theater
spectre	specter

Some exceptions are spelt the same in both languages, such as *acre, massacre, mediocre*, and *ogre*.

Some spellings are also flexible. In American English, *theatre* may be spelt both ways (though, again, this can depend on regions within the USA).

9.3.3 -s / -z / -c

Words that end in -**ise** or -**yse** in British English end in -**ize** or -**yze** in American English.

British English	American English
analyse	analyze
criticise	criticize
dramatise	dramatize
equalise	equalize
recognise	recognize
standardise	standardize

With words ending in -**ence** in British English, **s** may replace **c** in American English, for example *defence* (UK) / *defense* (US) and *offence* (UK) / *offense* (US).

Some verbs and nouns with the same spellings that both end in -ce in American English end in -se in British English for the verb form: *advise / advice, licence / license, practice / practise.*

9.3.4   -ogue / -og

Some nouns ending in -**ogue** in British English may end with -**og** or -**ogue** in American English (either form is correct, but should be used consistently).

British English	American English
analogue	analog / analogue
catalogue	catalog / catalogue
dialogue	dialog / dialogue
epilogue	epilog / epilogue
monologue	monolog / monologue
prologue	prolog / prologue

9.3.5   Double Vowels

Some words spelt with double vowels such as -**ae**- and -**oe**- in British English are spelt with -**e**- in American English.

British English	American English
foetus	fetus
leukaemia	leukemia
manoeuvre	maneuver
oestrogen	estrogen
paediatric	pediatric

9.3.6   Double Consonants

Some words that require a double consonant with a suffix in British English do not double the consonant in American English. See overleaf for a table of examples.

	British English	**American English**
cancel	cancelled	canceled
counsel	counsellor	counselor
equal	equalled	equaled
fuel	fuelling	fueling
jewel	jeweller	jeweler
marvel	marvellous	marvelous
model	modelling	modeling
travel	traveller	traveler

However, some words that end with a single **l** in British English end with a double **l** in American English, such as *appal* (UK) / *apall* (US), and *fulfil* (UK) / *fulfill* (US).

9.3.7 Past Tense Forms

In British English, some past forms of verbs use **-t** instead of **-ed**, while American English only uses the **-ed** ending. Many verbs may be spelt with either the **-ed** or **-t** ending in British English, but not in American English.

British English	**American English**
burned / burnt	burned
leaped / leapt	leaped
leaned / leant	leaned
learned / learnt	learned
smelled / smelt	smelled
spelled /spelt	spelled
spoiled / spoilt	spoiled

There are many rules that try to explain the differences, such as:

- American English uses the **-ed** form; British English uses **-t**.
- **-ed** is used for the simple past; **-t** is used for the past participle (perfect past).
- **-ed** is used for ongoing actions; **-t** for completed actions.

These rules all have exceptions, however, and you may find it to be simply a matter of style, depending on the region or the individual.

Another regional difference can be seen with certain past participles. In American English, some past participles end -**en** while in British English the verb form does not change from the past simple form, for example: *have got* (UK) / *have gotten* (US). American versions are often accepted in British writing, however, as the American usage is commonly understood.

9.3.8 Other Common Differences

There are a large number of additional minor differences in spelling between British and American English. In most cases, e.g. -**ou** / -**o** and -**ogue** / -**og**, this is where the older French or Latin spelling in British English is simplified in American English. Other common differences include: **ph** / **f**, e.g. *sulphur* (UK) / *sulfur* (US); **ough** / **f** or **w**, e.g. *plough* (UK) / *plow* (US); **que** or **q** / **ck**, e.g. *cheque* (UK) / *check* (US), **mme** / **m**, e.g. *programme* (UK) / *program* (US), and **y** / **i**, e.g. *tyre* (UK) / *tire* (US).

In addition to these patterns, there are also many individual spelling differences for specific words which do not necessarily fit a wider pattern. Examples include:

British English	American English
aluminium	aluminum
axe	ax
cosy	cozy
furore	furor
grey	gray
nought	naught
pyjamas	pajamas
sceptic	skeptic
whiskey	whisky

9.4 Tips for Spelling

Familiarising yourself with the rules and patterns in this chapter will help your spelling, but a good way to accurately learn words is to keep actively reading. If you read with a critical eye, you will pick out patterns yourself, and spot exceptions. There are exceptions everywhere, particularly as the lines between regional uses of English blur. If a spelling seems out of place or different to what you are used to, it is always worth questioning why.

Otherwise, accurate spelling comes from writing the words yourself, from memory when possible. Computer and phones now check spellings and offer suggestions, but try not to rely heavily on these tools. Using them to identify errors can be helpful, but using them to autocorrect your writing prevents you from learning the spelling yourself.

As much as possible, write for yourself and test your abilities. If the conditions of your writing do not allow for testing, such as when working to tight deadlines, set aside time separately. Attempt to write words from memory or transcribe audio sources. Test the phonetic sounds and spellings. Challenge yourself and you will improve.

10. Perspective

There are three main perspectives (or points of view) in writing. They are used in both fiction and non-fiction. Developing skills in writing different perspectives can help you to be more adaptable, as certain contexts can benefit from a different perspective.

Perspectives can be ordered by the distance they give the writer from a viewpoint. **First person** reports the writer's point of view (*me*), **second person** reports the reader's point of view (*you*), and **third person** reports a more neutral viewpoint, with or without insights into thoughts and feelings.

10.1 First Person

First person perspective uses the pronouns **I** / **me** / **mine** (singular) and **we** / **our** / **ours** (plural). In fiction this is presented in a character's voice; in non-fiction it represents the writer personally:

- I watched as the ship came into the harbour, and worried that Anne was not on board.
- We developed a prototype for a new kind of bicycle, and intend to test it in the market.

First person is often removed from academic and business writing, though ideas and events may be described from a personal perspective. Such writing is made neutral by writing in the passive voice:

- A prototype for a new kind of bicycle was developed with the intention of testing it in the market.

10.2 Second Person

Second person perspective uses the pronouns **you** / **your** / **yours** (singular and plural). Information is either given directly, such as in instructions or via narratives that place the reader in a situation:

- You will find the keys under the mat.
- You stand at the mouth of a cave, and have a decision to make. Will you go in and brave the beast's lair, or go home for tea?

10.3 Third Person

Third person perspective uses nouns and third person pronouns, **he** / **she** / **it** (singular) and **they** (plural), to describe events. It can vary in how subjective or distanced it is. The three main stances third person perspective takes are: **third person objective**, **third person limited**, and **third person omniscient** (there are other ways to describe third person narratives, but these are a good starting point).

Third person objective is a neutral description of events – providing no insight into internal feelings. This is commonly used in non-fiction; for example, reports and academic texts:

- The vets saved the kitten and celebrated by opening a bottle of champagne. *(no description of internal thoughts or feelings)*

Third person limited limits the text to information only available to one subject. This is common in fiction, keeping the reader's perspective close to a character's without actually telling a story in their own voice:

- Martin knocked on the door; he could hear someone laughing, far away. It was unsettling. *(In this example,* unsettling *is an insight into Martin's personal feelings in the situation.)*

Third person limited is less common in non-fiction, but may be used when reporting a situation where a restricted viewpoint was important, such as in an incident report detailing a particular perspective.

Third person omniscient describes events with an unlimited perspective, potentially offering full knowledge of a character's feelings, an in-depth topic, or a complex situation. This could take the form, for example, of a comprehensive non-fiction report, or of a narrative that describes information the characters do not all have access to themselves:

- Two suspects were arrested near the carnival tent, while the ringleader escaped on a scooter. *(two events described at the same time)*
- Martin waited for his wife to answer the door, unaware that she was preoccupied in the garden. *(Martin's activities described with reference to something he does not know)*
- Martin waited for his wife to answer the door, unsure if she was in. Betty busied herself in the garden, hoping Martin would just go away. *(two different character perspectives shown in one narrative)*

10.4 Non-fiction Perspectives

Typically, non-fiction is written in either the personal first person or the more official third person. You may be expected to use a certain perspective by your publication or audience. This may be decided for you by a company or publication style guide. Usually, a company or publisher (depending on its size) will make efforts to frame all its content in the same perspective, as part of an established image. If you have a choice, however, the following points should help you decide.

In the case of writing correspondence, such as emails and letters, it is natural to write in the first person. You are typically representing yourself, and it would be strange to present yourself otherwise. If you wish to write an email on behalf of your company, however, you need to consider whether the email is in the first person (plural) or third person:

- We are happy to announce the release of our flying car.
- SkyAuto are happy to announce the release of their flying car.

Here, first person sounds informal while third person sounds official. Both have their uses. The first person can build rapport and a relationship, which is good for engaging readers and encouraging action, while the third person creates distance, which is good for reporting news with a greater sense of importance. The first person is useful when putting on a friendly, human face while the third person can create a sense of a wider picture. The third person is also useful when you expect your writing to be reproduced. This is important when sending press releases, so publications can use your message without editing it.

In reports, articles, books and other work of longer, descriptive non-fiction, the **third person objective** or **omniscient** is typical when the topic being discussed is more important than the writer's viewpoint. Removing the writer's viewpoint stops the writer from becoming a distraction. This can make your writing more neutral, to help it appear objective and reliable. Consider how much more authority the second example has here:

- I tested the prediction model in three environments, with the same results.
- The prediction model was tested in three environments, with the same results.

This choice of perspective here is connected to using the passive voice, which is covered in more detail in **12.1 When to Use the Passive Voice**.

For marketing and related writing, when the goal is to generate an action, the choice of perspective may be more creative. Using an unexpected style may help a company to stand out or to specifically engage on a topic. For example, a large company might adopt the first person perspective to appear more friendly, or to take responsibility when breaking bad news.

Marketing and related writing is where you will commonly see the second person perspective (*you*) in writing. Writing in the second person engages the reader. Using a second person subject appeals to self-interest. Consider the different impact of these examples:

- I think this is a great product.
- You'll think this is a great product.

This speaks to people on a personal, motivating level. It can be used inspirationally, encouraging sales or other actions (*You have to buy this car!*), and it can be used within instructional texts, to demonstrate possibility and help engage the reader personally (as is used throughout this guide – *you can write this way, too*).

10.5 Fiction Perspectives

The choice between perspectives in fiction and creative writing is much more flexible and subjective than with non-fiction. It will depend on the nature of your narrative and the response you wish to get from your reader. To decide which perspective is best, these questions may help:

- Do you want to describe your character's innermost thoughts and feelings?
- Do you want to explore a particular viewpoint?
- Can you maintain a particular tone of voice (and will it be a good reading experience)?
- Can you tell your story effectively with the information that a particular perspective offers?

From there, you can consider each perspective in more detail to decide which is most appropriate. Note that second person and third person objective narratives are rare in creative writing, as addressing your reader directly or discussing neutral topics are less useful when you wish to engage them in a story.

10.5.1 First Person

First person perspective is the best choice for an intimate telling of a story, in a specific tone of voice. It limits the viewpoint for the purposes of information and tension, and makes it easier to explore your character's feelings. If you choose to write in the first person, the tips overleaf can help:

1. Maintain a consistent and realistic tone of voice, using **only** language that the narrator would use.
2. Never give information that the narrator is not aware of, which may include descriptions and explanations of things your character might not know, even as simple as the name of a bird, for example.
3. Consider how much is described. A narrator may give more or less information depending on the situation they are describing and how it personally moves them.
4. Consider the pace of your writing. A first person narrator is present throughout a story, making it important to plan breaks in the narrative.

10.5.2 Third Person Limited

In narrative fiction, the third person limited perspective offers a specific external viewpoint. Events are described in the third person, but the information provided is limited to what one character can see, and should only present information the character knows:

*   Gertrude pulled the lever, but the box didn't open. She couldn't see what was wrong. *(Third person limited: the character does not know the explanation.)*
*   Gertrude pulled the lever, but the box didn't open. The mechanism inside had snapped. *(Third person omniscient: the narrator gives information which the character cannot see.)*

When writing in the third person limited, consider what information you can include. Choose a particular character and imagine telling the story over their shoulder. You can go further than simply describing what they see, however; pay attention to what they think and feel.

Providing thoughts and feelings for the character can be done with varying levels of directness, including **direct** and **indirect reporting** and a method often called **free indirect style**.

The following examples demonstrate different ways the third person limited can present the thoughts of a character (Sally):

- As Bob described his plan to Sally, she kept quiet, thinking "What a terrible idea." *(direct speech for reporting thoughts, shown in quotes or, in some styles, italics)*
- As Bob described his plan to Sally, she kept quiet, thinking it was a terrible idea. *(indirect speech for reporting thoughts)*
- As Bob described his plan to Sally, she kept quiet. What a terrible idea. *(free indirect style)*

Free indirect style includes thoughts and feelings of the character as part of the narrative, essentially creating a mix between third and first person. Thoughts and feelings may be presented without quotation marks, though they should be clearly separated from the general narration; for example, appearing as separate sentences or with other appropriate punctuation.

Character thoughts presented in this way require practice. Watch out for clashing tenses, as a story told in the past tense may include character thoughts in the present tense, and the verbs can be confusing alongside each other. When verbs for character thoughts are included, it is best that the tense agrees with the narrative, to avoid confusing the reader (so the thought comes from the character but is not a direct quote):

- She opened the drawer and frowned, wondering, "Where's my diary?" *(direct quote of a thought)*
- She opened the drawer and frowned. Where was her diary? *(free indirect style, thought included as a narrative sentence)*

As well as including thoughts and feelings, the third person limited can also set a particular tone by using **only** the language of the character that's being followed:

- The witch-hunter stopped at the top of the hill, looking down at the disgusting, sinful village.

In the above example, the adjectives *disgusting* and *sinful* belong to the character. They are subjective adjectives for how he sees the village. This draws the narrative closer to the character, seamlessly presenting his attitudes. As well as demonstrating the character's thoughts, your choice of language might give insights into their background or education:

- The witch-hunter stopped at the top of the hill, looking down at the decayed village, a reprehensible place indeed.
- The witch-hunter stopped at the top of the hill, looking down at the dirty village, full of really bad people.

Our witch-hunter in the first example comes across as more educated, and perhaps pompous, while the simplistic vocabulary in the second example makes him seem uneducated.

When making such decisions, consistency is very important. Inconsistencies in the attitudes presented and language used will break the style, and you must be careful about the amount of information you show:

- Maurice read the sign with confusion. He had never seen this word before. *Taxidermy.* What did it mean?
- Maurice read the sign with confusion. He had never seen this word before. *Taxidermy.* He was not to know the office would contain dead animals. *(This goes too far, as it explains what the character does not know.)*

Another important consideration when writing in the third person limited is that we should never be told what another character thinks, feels, or sees. If you wish to give insights into a different character, it must be done through the main character's viewpoint. Do this with verbs that tell us, for example, how things *seem, appear,* or *look* to the main character. You may need to add additional details (such as body language indicators) to make this credible:

- Jim arrived at the party early. This was going to be great fun. When he saw Kylie come in, though, she had a scowl on her face that suggested she didn't feel the same way.

In this example, because we are writing from Jim's perspective, Kylie's attitude is shown through her scowl, and we use the verb *suggest* to give an idea of her viewpoint.

10.5.3 Third Person Omniscient

The third person omniscient perspective gives a global point of view. It can give a wider picture of events, without limiting us to what one character sees or thinks. It can be used to demonstrate multiple viewpoints within a scene, though this should be done with appropriate verbs for direct or indirect reporting, to avoid confusion:

- The Willis family entered the restaurant. Tracy loved this place, and took in the old Chinese lanterns fondly, but her sons thought it was tacky.

Multiple thoughts shown in this way would be inappropriate in third person limited. Even in third person omniscient, such examples are rare. Jumping between perspectives in a single scene, or a paragraph, is referred to as **head hopping**, and can easily become confusing or unsettling for readers:

- Jim arrived at the party early. This was going to be great fun. Kylie came in just behind him. It looked like a bore.

The example above quickly gives two perspectives, which would be confusing for the reader. An omniscient narrative works better as a series of limited passages, rather than flowing together like this. Third person omniscient may then separate points of views distinctly with a line break or other indicator that the narrative has been interrupted (e.g. *Kylie came in just behind him. To her, it looked more like a bore.*). Some writers advise that you only change perspective between chapters, which, strictly speaking, creates an omniscient story from a series of limited perspectives.

Third person omniscient can also be used to present information that the character does not know, which is useful for building tension and is sometimes necessary to help a reader understand a situation:

- Lana swam at full speed, determined to beat her record, completely unaware of the shark below her.
- Ted tossed more paper into the fire, in the hope of getting it going. He had no way of knowing that the scrap he'd mistaken for an old receipt was, in fact, the winning lottery ticket.

73

Though this technique has its specific uses, such details can be disorientating for a reader or break the flow of a narrative, so there are other ways to present these situations, with a limited perspective. In these examples, Lana could be surprised by a shark attack, or Ted could later realise his ticket had gone missing. Clues could also be left so that the reader might notice what the character doesn't (e.g. *Lana swam at full speed, ignoring the shadow-like form that was moving below her*). In such situations, the choice between third person limited and third person omniscient depends on how skilfully you can present these situations from one perspective or another, to give the reader the best experience.

Note also that though third person omniscient can present a wider scope than third person limited, it is still important to pay attention to the language you use. For an effective reading experience, the language and information presented should still be appropriate to the context of the story. Modern ideas in a historical story, for example, will break the atmosphere, even if you have an omniscient perspective.

11. Choice of Tense

English can be written in the past, present, and future tenses. Though there are many additional ways to define tenses for specific purposes, most writing is at least roughly framed in one of these three times. Broadly speaking, the **past tense** reports things that **were completed** in the past, the **present tense** reports things that **put the reader in the moment** or that have an **ongoing/timeless relevance**, and the future tense reports **what will happen**.

Consider your choice of tense before you start writing. Changing tense in the middle of a piece of writing creates an uncomfortable and confusing reading experience, and it is difficult to later edit a piece of writing from one tense to another without errors.

11.1 The Past

The past tense is a natural choice for storytelling and reporting as it refers to completed events. It particularly deals with events that **have happened**:

- We built a wall that kept the wild dogs out.
- The oldest Egyptian pyramid was built around 4,500 years ago.

If the described event has an ongoing impact or is relevant to the present or future, then the present perfect tense or the present tense start to become more useful:

- We have built a wall that keeps the wild dogs out. *(The action has happened, but the situation is ongoing: the wall keeps the dogs out for now...)*
- Our current historical data suggests that the oldest Egyptian pyramid was built around 4,500 years ago. *(The event is described in the past, but framed in the present, because the data continues to make this claim.)*

11.2 The Present

Writing in the present tense puts the reader in the moment. English speakers use present tense narratives in everyday speech to create a sense of immediacy in comic or dramatic storytelling. It can also be used to present an event as ongoing or rule-based, or to discuss ideas that are presented in other media (and continue to be presented each time that media is consumed). It is also common in interviews and travel writing, to set a particular scene.

The present tense is particularly useful when writing:

- CVs, cover letters, and skills profiles *(to demonstrate ongoing and currently relevant experience)*
- descriptions of anything that is true **now** *(such as when describing a location or an ongoing event)*
- advertising copy *(to create a living scene)*
- synopses of other media *(to explain ideas presented in books, films, articles, etc.)*
- instructions *(for actions to be followed as they are read)*

For example:

- Our company repairs computers.
- I'm fluent in ten programming languages.
- New York is a city of opportunity, where migrants continue to search for a new life.
- Zimbardo's *The Lucifer Effect* takes its title from an idea of how good men turn evil.
- Our paper explains the theory and methodology of the study, and the results demonstrate evidence to continue the research.
- Break the glass, pull the bell, and run for the fire door.

The use of the present tense may be required by certain style guides when writing for particular publications. Academic abstracts, for example, may be required to be in the present tense, though sometimes they are written in the past or future tense depending on the publisher.

11.3 The Future

The future tense is primarily used in writing to introduce upcoming ideas and events, for plans or for instructions. It can be written in a variety of forms, depending on the nature of the text. The **will** future form is commonly used for upcoming events or to confirm something that is soon to happen:

- This paper will document various plants that are found in the Lea Valley.
- The speaker will arrive at 9 a.m. and give his speech at 10 a.m. We will then reconvene for coffee.

In less formal writing, deciding on a future form may depend on the usual considerations for choosing the future tense, such as how recently or loosely plans have been made. The present tense may also be used for a future meaning with or without adding a time, depending on your context:

- I'm travelling into London, as the concert is being held in the Albert Hall. *(Informally discussing a planned event – the context lets us know the concert will occur in the future.)*

The present tense with a future meaning can also be used to save time and space if you are writing in a spreadsheet or time-line format, with the time stated separately. This may take the form of sentence fragments:

- Day 1 – Item goes on sale.
- Day 2 – Profits escalate.

11.4 Choosing the Best Tense

Every tense has its uses, so it's important to understand their benefits. Consider the impact of each sentence here, and when you would use them:

1. Our methods will never fail.
2. Our methods never fail.
3. Our methods have never failed.
4. Our methods never failed.

The examples variously emphasise (1) determination for the future, (2) timeless success, (3) a proven history of success, and (4) a historical account of success. The specific tense you choose may therefore depend on the purpose of your writing, as decided when you plan your text. This is one simple example of the differences between the tenses. There are many more considerations that will become more apparent with more reading and practice. The wider nuances of the English tenses are discussed in even more detail in my book, *The English Tenses Practical Grammar Guide*.

12. Passive and Active Writing

A common English writing tip is to write in the active voice whenever possible. This is the difference between assigning a verb to an actor (active) and saying that the action was done **to** something (passive).

- Trevor opened the door. *(active)*
- The door was opened. *(passive)*

Generally, the active voice is more direct and helps focus the action. The passive voice makes sentences longer and gives a more neutral perspective. In the above example, the active sentence creates a complete image, while the passive sentence is incomplete, hiding *who* opened the door and *how* it was done (i.e. by a person or some other force). Using active sentences helps keep your language clear and simple, as encouraged in George Orwell's rule:

- Never use the passive when you can use the active.

He does not simply say *never use the passive*. The passive voice has a number of important uses, so you must question when it is appropriate.

12.1 When to Use the Passive Voice

The passive voice is useful when we want to emphasise the object of a verb, or when the subject of the verb is either unimportant or more effectively left out. There are many reasons to do this, looked at in turn below.

12.1.1 Emphasising the Result of an Action

- Our windows were broken by the earthquake. *(The effect on the windows is more important than the cause.)*

12.1.2 When the Actor of the Verb Isn't Important

- The results will be made available in two weeks' time. *(The availability is important, not who makes them available.)*
- The data was cross-referenced against past results to demonstrate a positive increase. *(It does not matter who did this, only the results and the process used to obtain them.)*
- The police were called to the scene after neighbours were woken by the sound of gunfire. *(The focus is on how the event unfolded, not who called the police or shot the guns.)*

12.1.3 Deliberately Leaving Out Information

- She reached the car and gasped. The tyres had been slashed open. *(The mystery of who damaged the tyres adds suspense and tension.)*
- A mistake was made in the previous newsletter. *(With an unassigned action, we avoid directly blaming someone or personally taking responsibility.)*

12.1.4 Discussing General Truths

- Language is learnt from an early age. *(generally)*

One of the general applications of the passive voice is to emphasise results, when the result is more important than the subject:

- The team are working on the report. Bob will present it today.
- The team are working on the report. It will be presented today.

The first example emphasises who is presenting the report, while the second, with the passive voice, emphasises that the report is being presented. If the actor is not important, the passive voice puts focus on what is important.

The passive voice can also set a particular tone. It can sound more impersonal and neutral, which is useful for formal and polite sentences.

Active sentences, on the other hand, may too seem personal, or direct. Consider the following active sentences, and how they might be interpreted:

- You must do something to change this. *(personal threat)*
- We will mark the exams this weekend. *(taking personal responsibility)*

In the passive voice, these sound more neutral:

- Something must be done to change this. *(neutral assertion)*
- The exams will be marked this weekend. *(impersonal action)*

By removing the actor, we remove responsibility. The first sentence is no longer direct or personal because **by who** is not emphasised. The second sentence no longer says who will mark the exams, which makes it more neutral. Such neutral sentences can sound more professional and build confidence that a task will be done without inviting the reader to consider how. Such considerations for setting this particular tone are covered in more detail in **13.1 The Passive Voice in Formal Language**.

12.2 Avoiding the Passive Voice

Passive sentences often creep into writing unintentionally, without fitting any of the purposes listed above. When you understand the particular uses of the passive voice, you can start removing unnecessary passive sentences:

- The letter was received by Wendy.
- Wendy received the letter.

Here, the amount of information available is the same in both sentences. The main reason to use the passive would be to focus on the letter; for example, to highlight it in contrast to another object, or to highlight what became of it:

- The letter was received by Wendy, but she never got the email.
- The letter, which they thought had been lost at sea, was actually received by Wendy.

If the sentence is not being used for such purposes, then the active version is more direct and shorter, without changing the meaning. In this way, the active voice can make writing clearer and easier to read.

In other examples, the passive voice may avoid giving complete information, either because it is unknown or unwanted. When this information is important, it can lead to sentences that lack confidence or authority, reducing credibility:

- A study was conducted into sleep deprivation. *(By not stating who did it, the reader may think you are not fully informed.)*
- I'm sorry the information was lost. *(By not stating who lost the information, the statement avoids responsibility and may not be considered genuine.)*

There are two techniques you can use to identify passive sentences, so you can find them and question their validity.

First, search for sentences that use the verb **to be** (*am, is, are, was, were*). These may be stative (*I was hungry.*) or continuous (*They were calling for help.*), so also look for a **past participle**. You can quickly identify passive constructions this way:

- The report **was filed** by the receptionist.
- The duck **was eaten** by a lion.
- Fred and Sonya **were** being **watched**.

Second, check for meaning in the sentence. Can we ask *by whom/what?*

- The glass was broken. *(By whom? It doesn't say.)*
- The fire was started by the janitor. *(By whom? The janitor – not the subject.)*

This second method of identifying passive sentences is also a useful way of deciding whether or not the sentence belongs in the passive. The importance of the answer can tell you how effective the active voice would be. In the examples above, the importance of the answers depends on the purpose of the sentences. Are we trying to identify how the window was broken or who started the fire, or is it not the main point of the sentence?

With a little more context the effectiveness of the passive or active voice can become clearer.

- We could not see through the window because the glass was broken. *(By whom? It does not matter here, because we are discussing the ability to see through it.)*
- Billy threw the ball clumsily and the glass was broken. *(By who? Billy; we know this and assigning the active verb to him will create a simpler, more direct sentence.)*

There are also times when the actor may still be important but we deliberately want to delay assigning the action to him. This can be because another action in the sentence is more important, or to delay revealing something, for example:

- It took them two hours to put out the fire, which was started by the janitor. *(Though it is still important to report who started it, the initial emphasis on this sentence is how it was dealt with.)*
- "Young Frederick was not responsible for this tragedy – the fire was started by... the janitor!" *(delaying for dramatic effect)*

These considerations show how writing in the active or passive voice can be a matter of style. Use your judgement to decide what the best choice is for each sentence. In general, the active voice helps create clearer, more direct writing, but in some contexts the passive voice will have a specific and effective job to do.

13. Formal Language

Formal writing is commonly found in academic and business writing, and in correspondence that needs to demonstrate respect. Written English is generally more formal than spoken English, as it is possible to edit writing and present more accurate language.

Following the principle of writing clearly and simply, you will find that most of your writing can already be read in a formal and respectful manner. In cases when you want to be particularly formal, however, there are two key techniques that will help. Firstly, you can **use the passive voice**. Secondly, you can **use formal vocabulary**. Both techniques should be used in moderation, however, as overly complex sentences and vocabulary can become unclear.

13.1 The Passive Voice in Formal Language

The passive voice is particularly useful in formal writing for instructions or general announcements, where the subject is less important than the result:

- Workers will be paid at the end of the month.

As discussed in **12. Passive and Active Writing**, processes described in the passive voice remove the actor, making texts more neutral and unemotional. This can be used to avoid being personal or to indirectly assign an action (where emphasising the actor might seem blunt or lack subtlety):

- Dinner is served in the canteen.
- The study was successfully completed by researchers from three different departments.
- We are humbled by your presence. *("Your presence humbles us." would be very direct.)*

The active voice is still important in formal writing if you want your writing to sound personal, or you want to take responsibility for something:

- You will be paid at the end of the week.
  → We will pay you at the end of the week. *(taking responsibility)*

Combining active and passive can therefore help separate neutral and personal statements. In the space of one sentence you can, for example, use two tones: one, in the passive, to provide a neutral and formal statement (emphasising an action's completion) and another, in the active, to emphasise agency or opinion:

- The remaining balance will be paid at the end of the week – we will make sure of it.

In this example, the writer keeps the payment neutral to remove any doubt about the action being completed, followed by an emphatic personal assurance in the active. It is important to create such a balance between neutrality/respect and agency/emotion in formal writing. Carefully placed active phrases can help personalise and humanise otherwise neutral writing.

Using the passive or active voice alone will not determine if a text is formal or informal, however. A completely active text may still be formal, with the right choice of vocabulary, and may be preferable if the specific effects of the passive voice are not required.

13.2 Formal Vocabulary

As discussed in **7. Vocabulary**, the English language includes many words that mean the same thing, with some versions considered more formal than others. It is often possible to make your writing more formal by using the French equivalents of common Old English words (e.g. *chauffeur* vs *driver*, *discuss* vs *chat*). See **7.3 Synonyms** for more examples.

Formal English should also **avoid phrasal verbs**, which are generally considered informal. The following examples demonstrate an informal (more personal, lighter) tone, because of the phrasal verbs:

- I dropped off the samples in the morning.
- Tidy up the report before going home.

It is generally possible to find a more formal equivalent of a phrasal verb. To find phrasal verbs in your writing, look for verbs that are joined by a participle (which looks like a preposition), or look for verbs formed from more than one word. See if you can think of a single-word equivalent:

- I **dropped off** the samples at Dr Brown's office. *(informal phrasal verb)*
- I **deposited/delivered** the samples to Dr Brown. *(formal verbs)*
- I **left** the samples with Dr Brown. *(neutral verb)*

By choosing your words carefully, you can give a text varying levels of formality, as required. Exactly how formal you wish to be will depend on your text. In different contexts, a more formal or a less formal style may be required. The full range can be seen in British newspapers, for example: they may be very formal and contain a high level of vocabulary (such as in certain broadsheets); they may be more neutral with some more casual language (as found in popular daily papers); or they may be informal and contain very colloquial language (as seen in the tabloids). Bear in mind these papers choose their different vocabulary to appeal to different audiences, and your writing should be done with the same consideration in mind. Without a specific reason to use a different verb, our example above would be most accessible (and clear and simple) using the neutral verb, *left*.

13.3 Salutations and Valedictions

Salutations and valedictions, the opening and closing comments of a letter (or other correspondence), are particular signals for formality in writing. There is a wide range of choices for opening and closing correspondence, often used in matching pairs. Historically, with letter-writing, these were used in specific circumstances, but in modern usage, as email has encouraged more casual writing, these conventions have become more casual, too.

Salutations are typically a word or phrase followed by a name. A common salutation is *Dear ...*, though in informal or impersonal use, *To ...*, is sometimes used. In email and other electronic correspondence, it has become acceptable to open messages with various other greetings, as with spoken English, the most common being *Hello* and, less formally, *Hi*.

Salutations are typically followed by an honorific (title) and a surname, followed by a comma:

- Dear Mr Willis,
- To Dr Reed,

The abbreviated honorific may be followed by a period *(Mr., Mrs., Dr.)* in US English, but the full stop is typically left out in modern British English. Choosing the correct honorific is important to show the correct level of respect. Typically, people go by their highest level of title (e.g. a professor would not be addressed as *Dr* or *Mr*).

Honorifics are historically gendered in English, which can be controversial: *Mrs* refers to a married woman and *Miss* refers to a young or unmarried woman. To avoid this labelling, the neutral *Ms* is used, and a gender-neutral alternative is also possible, *Mx*. In very formal English, *Mesdames* may be used to address a collective group of women, and *Messieurs* (or its abbreviation, *Messrs*) to address a group of men.

The honorific may be written in full, though this is usually only done for professional titles and dignitaries (e.g. *Professor Smith, Madam President*). Writing a professional title in full is another way to add formality.

A salutation may be followed by a first name, instead of the surname, which is generally more casual and informal. Honorifics are not typically used with a first name (though they may be, with professional titles):

- Dear Paula,
- To Richard,
- Hi Charlene,

Full names are rarely written in a salutation. Sometimes, however, the salutation is dropped, in particularly formal greetings (sounding very direct):

Sirs/Madams,

We kindly request that you return your dinnerware to the appropriate station.

Or in particularly informal greetings (sounding brief and friendly):

Harry –
Let's meet up this evening!

If you don't know the name of the person you are addressing, it is typical to write *Sir or Madam* instead of a name (used together if you don't know the recipient's gender). *To Whom it May Concern* may also be used to start a letter where the name is not known, with the implication that it may be passed on to the most relevant contact.

Valedictions, or complimentary closes, are more flexible and numerous than salutations, particularly in casual correspondence. Most commonly, and formally, letters end with *Yours sincerely,* (if you know the recipient's name) or *Yours faithfully,* (if you do not know the recipient's name). A wide variety of alternatives are available, however, with various degrees of formality:

- Yours truly, *(formal and impersonal)*
- Yours respectfully, / Respectfully yours, *(formal, acknowledging authority)*
- Sincerely yours, / Sincerely, *(less formal, more personal)*
- Cordially, *(less formal)*
- Kind regards, / Best regards, / Personal regards, / Kindest regards, / Warmest regards, / Regards, / Best wishes, *(informal, more personal)*

Other variations include more informal abbreviated versions, such as *Yours,* or *Best,* which show a high degree of familiarity. Other adjectives may also be used (with or without *Yours …*), expressing particular emotions, such as *hopefully* or *lovingly.* There are many more alternatives that may be entirely unique to the writer.

For the purposes of formal writing, be aware that standard salutations and valedictions will be expected. Writing with less formal and alternative variations is a matter of style, however, and such phrases can be adopted and adapted depending on what you are writing.

13.4 The Right Level of Formality

The purpose of your writing may dictate how formal you wish to make it. You may wish to command respect and authority (e.g. in a disciplinary message to your employees), or you may wish to show empathy and a personal touch (e.g. in a holiday greeting or in response to a crisis). A little informal language, such as strategically placed active phrases and informal vocabulary, can add a human touch to otherwise formal writing. However, a human touch in a scientific paper, for example, can appear inappropriate.

Formal language creates technical, unfeeling writing – the language of important or unemotional tasks. Perhaps the best way to view it is to ask yourself: how much feeling do you wish to show in your writing, and exactly what kind of feeling do you wish to demonstrate?

- Collect your new pass from reception. *(formal, neutral)*
- Pick up your new pass from reception. *(informal, familiar)*
- Your pass is waiting in reception. *(formal, cold)*

The simple comparison above demonstrates the subtle difference between formal and informal language. How important this is, and if it will be noticed, depends on your context. In certain circumstances, any of these sentences might be used with little difference. In other contexts, such language must be chosen carefully. In a welcoming email for a conference, for example, the informal example may be accepted as a light and friendly introduction, but as a set of instructions offered to a highly respected visiting ambassador, it may seem disrespectful.

14. Emphasis

Many of the exceptions to grammatical rules in English relate to emphasising particular words or ideas. Emphasis can affect structure, word order, vocabulary choice, formatting and punctuation. The examples below show some of the ways one sentence or idea can be changed for emphasis:

- The man opened the door using a hammer.
- Using a hammer, the man opened the door.
- The man smashed the door in with a hammer.
- The man opened the door using a *hammer*.
- The door was opened with a hammer.

Considerations for emphasis appear throughout this book, but this section specifically looks at some of the most common methods.

14.1 Punctuation and Formatting

The simplest way to add emphasis in writing is to use punctuation, such as the exclamation point (!), or formatting, such as using *italics*. Other techniques include using abbreviations, contractions, and interjections.

14.1.1 The Exclamation Point

The **exclamation point** is typically used to demonstrate emotion, such as surprise or anger:

- The results were in. She had won by one vote!

Exclamation points lose their impact if used too often, and can look amateurish in narrative prose and non-fiction, as it shows a reliance on punctuation rather than language. The exclamation point is useful in dialogue, though, to demonstrate emotion. The following two examples create very different tones:

- "What are you doing?" he asked. "You're not allowed in here."
- "What are you doing?" he asked. "You're not allowed in here!"

The exclamation point makes the difference between a calm, uncertain statement and a more emotional, shocked response. When using an exclamation point, ask yourself if it has a similar impact on your overall tone, to see if it is necessary. Note, though, it can affect the tone in different ways. Another common use of the exclamation point is to highlight informal or surprising information, particularly in casual correspondence:

- It was good to see you last night; I can't believe how much we drank. *(appears unemotional, even sarcastic)*
- It was good to see you last night; I can't believe how much we drank! *(emphasises surprise and sets a lighter tone)*

14.1.2 Italics

Italics (and alternative formatting techniques) draw attention to a particular word or phrase. When we stress a word in a sentence, it can change the way the whole sentence is read. A common expressive exercise in spoken English (often used in acting classes) is to repeat a single sentence with the stress on a different word. This produces very different tones. The same is true in writing; using *italics* can stress one word or phrase, drawing attention to it and encouraging a particular interpretation of the sentence:

- We only work on Wednesdays, and we don't repair computers.
- We *only* work on Wednesdays, and we don't repair computers. *(emphasising the limited time-frame)*
- We only work on *Wednesdays*, and we don't repair computers. *(emphasising the specific day)*
- We only work on Wednesdays, *and* we don't repair computers. *(emphasising there are two things to be clarified)*

- We only work on Wednesdays, and we *don't* repair computers. *(emphasising the second point as particularly striking; perhaps the suggestion is offensive)*
- We only work on Wednesdays, and we don't *repair* computers. *(emphasising the action, to suggest they do something else relating to computers)*
- We only work on Wednesdays, and we don't repair *computers*. *(emphasising the object, to suggest they repair something else)*

Alternatives to emphatic *italics* may depend on the style of a particular text or publication. Some texts use **bold**, <u>underlining</u> or CAPITALS instead of *italics*. This has become particularly flexible online, as writers look for different techniques to make words stand out. There is no single correct style, but it is important to be consistent.

14.1.3 Abbreviations, Contractions, and Interjections

Another way to add emphasis is by expanding on abbreviations or contractions. If we do not use a contraction where one might be expected (such as in casual writing and dialogue), the contracted word can stand out. This can be combined with italics for additional emphasis:

- We don't repair computers.
- We do not repair computers.
- We do *not* repair computers.

Commas can be used in a similar way to emphasise a particular word or phrase as an **interjection**, slowing a sentence down and making a word or phrase stand out. We do this with parenthetical commas, which can be used to interject a word or phrase in various places in a text. It can also be done with dashes instead of commas. This is covered in more detail in the following sections, but is worth noting here as it emphasises adverbs and adjectives in the same way as *italics* and the other formatting alternatives:

- We ran terrified through the house.
- We ran, terrified, through the house.
- We ran – terrified – through the house.

14.2 Structural Emphasis

If your writing is structured regularly, with paragraphs and sentences of typical lengths, then any break in the pattern can add emphasis. The following tips are mostly useful for narratives, as more formal writing is likely to be more clear and convincing following standard structures. Depending on your purposes, these techniques may also be applied in other fields.

An occasional short sentence is useful to break up blocks of text when you want to draw attention to a particular piece of information, or for dramatic effect:

> There will be no football practice on Monday as we are filling holes in the pitch. Practice will resume as usual on Tuesday, however.
>
> Be there.

The above example makes its closing comment surprisingly forceful by being short and separate from the main body of text. The following example uses the same technique to create a softer, satisfying close:

> Harriet had been climbing the hill for hours. She'd passed through thick, spiky woodland and waded through a cold river. She'd climbed over a rock twice her height, and fended off a vicious raccoon. She reached the peak just after noon and finally rested.
>
> The view was worth it.

Using a short sentence to provide emphasis and structural variety can also be effective in the middle of a paragraph:

> He was sorting through the files in the attic when he found the one he was looking for. Evidence at last. The papers proved exactly what the old lady in the market had told him.

Such short sentences can highlight particular emotions or ideas. They could also be used to draw attention to a critical point of information:

> There was a sign on the door when the children arrived; the cameras show that the wording was clearly visible. No Entry. The children knew they should not have gone in, it was as plain as day.

This can be taken to a greater extreme with paragraphing. A single sentence can break up text dramatically by emphasising a specific action or detail:

> Curtis washed windows for every house on the street except Number 32. Curtis had watched the house while he was working the road, hoping for a chance to say hello and offer his services. They never answered the door when he came calling. Their windows were filthy, though – you couldn't see through them.
>
> Finally, after six months of waiting, the door to Number 32 creaked open while Curtis watched from Number 38.
>
> He stopped dead in his tracks.
>
> He saw, then, why the couple in Number 32 were not interested in hiring a window cleaner. Both of them, the man and the woman, were carrying buckets and extendable mops. And on their shirts were the logos of Spotless Windows Limited.
>
> They were *the competition.*
>
> But why hadn't they cleaned their own windows?

There are four very short paragraphs here, two in the middle and two at the end. The ones in the middle give us a pause, adding tension to the rambling tale. The final sentences give us a dramatic realisation and the character's continuing thought process.

This passage uses a few other techniques to add emphasis and make the text more dramatic. **Italics** emphasise the words *the competition.* **Repetition** is used with *Both of them, the man and the woman,* which has the effect of explaining who *both of them* were and emphasises that it was true for two people, of two genders. There is a **dash** to emphasise related information: *Their windows were filthy, though – you couldn't see through them.* This could also be done with a semi-colon, as the two clauses are closely connected. Finally, commas are used to emphasise an adverb: *He saw, then.* This gives the character (and reader) a dramatic pause in the realisation.

Additional information can be added in many places in a sentence, to tell us something when it is most striking (continued opposite):

- The trees, blue and purple all over, did not look healthy.
- She finished the papers, all the papers, by nightfall.

Be careful not to over-complicate the sentence, though. Adding emphasis this way may break the flow, or reduce clarity:

- She finished the papers, which had been weighing on her mind for days and seemed like they would never end, by nightfall. *(too much information, losing the impact and splitting the sentence in an unclear way)*

If your writing has lots of short and clear sentences or paragraphs, however, you may find it possible to add emphasis with longer sentences. In the example below, the final sentence builds a sense of excitement after many short, neutral statements:

Barry was only six. He did not know much. He could not count past twenty. One thing he did know, though, was that the brand new Intergalactic Space Fleet Ray Gun would be his by the end of the week.

This example includes another useful emphasis technique, leading with the most important information: *One thing he did know* instead of *He did know one thing*. The following section discusses front-loading in detail for individual sentences, but it is worth considering on a wider structural level, too, as you may wish to add emphasis by moving a sentence within a paragraph. Consider our earlier example:

There was a sign on the door when the children arrived; the cameras show that the wording was clearly visible. No Entry. The children knew they should not have gone in, it was as plain as day.

This could be rearranged to lead with the words on the sign, throwing us right into the detail:

No Entry. The sign was on the door when the children arrived; the cameras show that the wording was clearly visible. The children knew, plain as day, they should not have gone in.

14.3 Rearranging Sentences

Placing information earlier in a sentence or clause typically emphasises it, which is useful for framing your text. For example, in a story, it may be important to know a character has a tool before we see them using it:

- Wielding a hammer, the man broke through the door.

Sentences are typically rearranged in this way using adverbials or prepositional phrases that put information such as times, manners, objects, and locations before the subject and action. The phrase is moved forward and separated by a comma:

- We'll be there by dinner time. → *By dinner time, we'll be there.*
- She ate the soup messily. → *Messily, she ate the soup.*
- He pried open the box with a knife.
  → *With a knife, he pried open the box.*
- They exchanged briefcases in a dark underpass.
  → *In a dark underpass, they exchanged briefcases.*

Longer phrases or clauses can draw particular attention to such ideas:

- By the time you've cooked dinner, we'll be there.
- With messy flicks of the spoon and smacking lips, she ate the soup.
- Using his favourite pocket knife, he pried open the box.
- Under the noisy road, watched by the rats, they exchanged briefcases.

Rearranging clauses is often taught with complex sentences, where either the dependent or independent clause can come first:

- The game may be cancelled, depending on the weather.
- Depending on the weather, the game may be cancelled.

In the first sentence, the possibility of cancelling the game is emphasised. The second sentence emphasises the weather's role in the decision.

With shorter sentences, there may not be a simple option for reordering the words to add emphasis, but it may still be possible by making slight alterations elsewhere. For example, changing to the passive voice can help to place the object at the beginning of a sentence:

- He knew one thing about girls. *(active)*
- There was one thing he knew about girls. *(passive, emphasising the definitive, singular thing)*

14.4 Repetition for Emphasis

Repetition of words and phrases can add emphasis in many ways. Throughout a text, repeated describing words and phrases (or using very similar describing words and phrases) can help set an overall tone or bring to mind a certain image. For example, repeated words, phrases, or ideas that relate to a particular colour can add a certain tint to your writing:

- The bedsheets were blue and the cabinet was the colour of dirty sea-water. The light reflected off marine walls.

This example uses subtly different repetition of a similar (blue) shade.

Repetition of different word types draws attention to their function. The sets of examples that follow in this section will show how short sentences can use repetition, quickly repeating a chosen idea. This can be expanded more generally with repetition over longer texts.

Repeated nouns, or **repeated pronouns**, emphasise a particular person or thing. This can draw attention to **who/what** is doing an action, it can draw particular attention to something, and in some cases it can demonstrate emotions associated with repetition, such as isolation or determination (see overleaf):

- Riley stormed into the kitchen. Riley took the cakes and Riley ate them all herself. *(emphasising who is to blame)*
- It was the candle that started the fire. The candle from the front room, the same candle that you told me never to throw away. The candle that smelt like cheese – the candle I never wanted. *(emphasising an emotional connection to a particular object)*

- I trekked for two hours through the jungle before I found a place to set up my camp. I erected the tent myself and I spent the next two hours searching for water. I found none. *(emphasising isolation through repeated personal pronouns)*
- Finn took the javelin. He looked at it, and he knew what he had to do. He would throw it further than anyone. He would be the champion. *(emphasising determination through repeating "he")*

Repeated verbs emphasise a continuing action. This can show that something is done over a long time, or that a task is repetitive:

- We ran through the town, we ran through the hills, we ran over the bridge and we ran all the way past the castle. *(emphasising the endurance of a long, ongoing action)*
- I cooked dinner every night. I cooked for the children and I cooked for my husband. I cooked when I wasn't feeling well. I even cooked when I had other places to be. *(emphasising the personally tedious activity, combined with repeated personal pronouns)*

Repeated prepositions emphasise objects' relationships to each other:

- The papers were in the office, in the drawer in your desk. *(emphasising awareness of an object's specific location)*
- She made the blanket with the family loom, with her own materials and within her own home. *(emphasising the character's independence through her situation and tools)*

Repeated adverbs or adverbials emphasise how something is done, usually drawing particular attention to timing or manner:

- He quickly opened the door, quickly threw off his shoes, quickly turned on the TV, and finally watched the news.
- The diamond was stolen at night. It was moved through the city at night and it left the country by boat at night. No one saw a thing. *(emphasising that the time was the reason no one saw it)*

These are just some of the examples of how repeated words can be used for emphasis. The uses are flexible and not limited to these ideas. Over longer texts, repetition may, for example, build character mannerisms or demonstrate consistency in activities. However, remember that repetition is often advised against in writing, and when used inappropriately it can be seen as clumsy. To make emphatic repetition effective, repetition must be used rarely and deliberately, as discussed in **7.4 Avoiding Repetition**.

14.5 Other Emphasis Techniques

There are many other techniques that can be used to add emphasis in writing, some more common (and accepted) than others. This can be as simple as demonstrating possession through a preposition rather than an apostrophe (*Knights of the Realm* rather than *the Realm's Knights*), or it can be as complex as emphasising an idea through repeated hints (for example, making references to boats throughout a mystery that reveals a murderous sailor).

One thing that all of these techniques have in common is that they only work when they are **exceptions** to the typical style, used **strategically**. Used too often, they lose their effect; used inappropriately, they can look like mistakes. A passage with too many stressed words can be confusing to read, and repetition that does not connect a clear idea looks lazy:

- There were *two* jars on the table when I left. *Now* there is only one. Who is *responsible* for this? *(This creates an odd rhythm.)*
- Gertrude lived in a big house, where she had a number of wardrobes for her big shoes and held lots of big parties. *("Big" does not emphasise one overall size here, as it refers to many things that are difficult to compare/combine.)*

The effectiveness of different emphasis techniques may also depend on the text itself, and its context and style requirements. For example, exclamation points will mostly look out of place in an academic paper, while advanced vocabulary can create an effective contrast to simple vocabulary. On the other hand, overly complex sentences or carefully rearranged paragraphs may interrupt readers in light fiction, while exclamation points could create simple, clear emphasis.

15. Punctuation

The most important purpose of accurate punctuation is to clarify sentences and avoid misunderstandings. This is a vast topic, and depending on who you are writing for, it may be worth investing in a style guide to cover all the potential considerations for punctuation, including regional variations.

In the US, *The Chicago Manual of Style* (University of Chicago, 2017) is a good starting point, while in the UK, with some different conventions, *New Hart's Rules: The Oxford Style Guide* (Waddingham, 2014) is one of the most popular guides. Be aware that publications, organisations, and individuals may put a heavy emphasis on specific punctuation conventions that are not taught as definitive rules. For example, academic journals are often particular about the position of commas and periods in references, though one journal's style may differ to another's.

This chapter covers the most common areas of confusion, which can be generally agreed upon with some exceptions.

15.1 Apostrophes

Apostrophes usually demonstrate either **possession** or **abbreviations**.

15.1.1 Apostrophes Demonstrating Possession

Possessive apostrophes are added with an **s** to most nouns. There are various rules for whether or not to add the extra **s** to words already ending in **s**, which can depend on style or personal preference. A good test is to try and pronounce the word. If it isn't easy to say with an extra **s**, don't add one:

- the computer → the computer**'s**
- Jess → Jess**'s**
- the huntresses → the huntresses**'**

Possessive apostrophes indicate possession of the following noun or phrase:

- The government**'s** problem.
- The huntresses**'** bows.

They are often used when discussing time:

- in ten years**'** time
- in a decade**'s** time

The possessive apostrophe is **not** added to possessive pronouns: *my, yours, his, hers, its, ours, theirs*.

15.1.2 Apostrophes Demonstrating Abbreviation

Abbreviating apostrophes are used to replace missing letters. These are often used for combining **to be** or **to have** with a noun or pronoun, or to combine **not** with a verb.

- I am fed up with this. → I**'m** fed up with this.
- He is funny. → He**'s** funny.
- She would have eaten that. → She would**'ve** eaten that.
- It was not a good idea. → It was**n't** a good idea.
- They could not start the car. → They could**n't** start the car.

Contractions are considered informal, so be wary of using them in written English. Most formal writing does not use contractions, though they may be acceptable in informal correspondence and written dialogue.

Abbreviating apostrophes are also used to shorten words for simpler or colloquial use:

- the 1970s → the '70s
- Vietnam → 'Nam *(colloquially used in the context of the war)*

Apostrophes are also commonly used with plurals. This is often a mistake, such as adding an apostrophe when adding a plural **s** *(I'm selling banana's!)*. In some cases, however, this is done to avoid confusion, particularly when dealing with single letters or words that are not commonly used as nouns:

- Mind your p's and q's.

The common expression in this example refers to letters, which are not typically recognised as nouns. It would be less clear without apostrophes: *mind your ps and qs*.

Using apostrophes with plurals in this way may be acceptable or not depending on the situation and you may be advised for or against their use by particular style guides. If in doubt, it may be best to rewrite your sentence, or consider using other punctuation or formatting to demonstrate an uncommon word or phrase:

- After five failed weddings, she had said a lot of I do's.
- After five failed weddings, she had said a lot of "I do"s.
- After five failed weddings, she had said a lot of *I dos*.
- After five failed weddings, she had said "I do" a lot.

15.2 Commas

Commas separate different parts of a sentence. Their main function is to make sentences clearer, by grouping words, phrases, and clauses. They can separate clauses, separate direct speech, mark off parts of a sentence (like parentheses), and separate adverbial phrases.

Commas may sometimes be used flexibly, depending on the sentence (though remember they are there to add clarity), and deviations from typical conventions can be distracting and confusing. A good question to ask when considering if a comma is necessary or not is: **is it easier to read the sentence with or without a comma?** The option less likely to confuse or interrupt your reader is best, which is true of most writing rules.

15.2.1 Separating Clauses

Commas separate clauses in complex sentences, when we have a main clause and one or more subordinate clauses:

- The passengers waited outside, while the steward refused to open the door.

The comma comes at the end of the first clause. In regular sentence structure, the comma often comes before a conjunction or other linking word. When complex sentences are reversed, with the linking word at the start of the sentence, the comma comes at the end of the first clause.

- While the steward refused to open the door, the passengers waited outside.

Commas in complex sentences are sometimes seen as optional, as the comma often has little impact on the meaning or understanding of the sentence. This can depend on the sentence itself, as commas between clauses are less necessary in shorter sentences or sentences where the clauses are more directly connected:

- They ate the cake before she could stop them.

With longer sentences, and sentences where the co-ordinating conjunction might create confusion with another noun, a comma can have a big impact on the meaning. This is particularly true with conjunctions like *as* and *while*, which could be interpreted as either *for the purposes of* or *at the same time as*:

- The accountant demanded a new lamp, as the dim light made work impossible. *(because working was impossible)*
- The accountant demanded a new lamp as the dim light made work impossible. *(The demand was made at the same time as the light worsened.)*

Commas are essential with particular types of subordinate clauses, such as non-defining relative clauses. Relative clauses, separated by the words

103

who, whom, that, and *which*, may include defining information (with no commas) or additional information (with the clause separated by commas).

- The man who had stolen the mango was imprisoned.
- The man, who had stolen the mango, was imprisoned.

In the above example, the first sentence tells us this particular man (the one responsible for the crime, not someone else) was imprisoned. The second sentence tells us a man was imprisoned who happened to commit this crime. In the first sentence, the relative clause (*who had stolen the mango*) is used as an identifying cause of imprisonment; in the second sentence, it is additional information, not necessarily the cause of imprisonment (the clause may be confirming that he was guilty, for example). This is a subtle example. How much difference the commas make with relative clauses may vary depending on the situation:

- The team who wanted the prize most won. *(They won because of their passion.)*
- The team, who wanted the prize most, won. *(They won and also had the most passion.)*
- Visitors that require special assistance should contact the front desk. *(only those who require assistance should contact the desk)*
- Visitors, who require special assistance, should contact the front desk. *(suggesting all visitors require special assistance)*

This use of commas overlaps with considerations for separating additional information within a sentence, which is covered in the section **15.2.4 Separating Information**.

15.2.2 Lists and the Serial Comma

Commas are used to separate items in lists of three or more words. This can apply to lists of different kinds of words, including lists of nouns, verbs, adjectives, and adverbs.

- We ate cheese, ham, and tomatoes. *(nouns)*
- On Saturday, Doris read, swam, and rested. *(verbs)*

- They bought a new, tall, glass door. *(adjectives)*
- Slowly, carefully, and deliberately, she opened the metal box. *(adverbs)*

Lists may or may not have a comma placed before the co-ordinating conjunction (*and*). This is called the **serial comma**, the **Oxford comma** or **Harvard comma**. Some English speakers argue that it is necessary while others believe it should be omitted. The truth lies somewhere in between:

- A Full English breakfast consists of eggs, beans, sausages, and bacon. *(serial comma)*
- A Full English breakfast consists of eggs, beans, sausages and bacon. *(no serial comma)*

In the above example, adding or removing the comma is unlikely to make any difference to how the sentence is understood. In can be argued, however, that in different contexts it may add or remove clarity. In the following sentences, the comma makes it clear how many items are in the list:

- We ate ham, tomatoes, and eggs. *(Comma separates three different food types.)*
- We ate ham, tomatoes and eggs. *(No comma leaves the possibility that the three foods were combined.)*
- Dedicated to my co-workers, Paul and Jim. *(No comma suggests Paul and Jim are the co-workers.)*
- Dedicated to my co-workers, Paul, and Jim. *(Comma suggests Paul and Jim are thanked in addition to the co-workers.)*

The serial comma can cause confusion, however, when it makes an item in a list appear to be additional information:

- The group included a doctor, Jim Smith, and a baker. *(suggesting the doctor is called Jim Smith)*
- The group included a doctor, Jim Smith and a baker. *(suggesting Jim Smith is a third member of the group)*

The particular cases for using the serial comma can depend entirely on the sentence: as these examples illustrate, it can sometimes remove ambiguity and can sometimes cause ambiguity. Generally, the serial comma is encouraged by the majority of American style guides and some British style guides. In-house guides or publications may either encourage or discourage it, so it is worth knowing what is acceptable for your particular piece of writing. However, this is a rare case where consistency is not always the best policy. The demands of a particular list may make the serial comma more or less useful.

In cases where the meaning appears to change with or without the comma, and neither is fully clear, it may be best to reword the sentence. In the examples below, neither option is clear:

- Mary travelled to New York with Jim Smith, a doctor and a scholar. *(Is Jim Smith both a doctor and a scholar, or did Mary travel with three people?)*
- Mary travelled to New York with Jim Smith, a doctor, and a scholar. *(Is Jim Smith a doctor or did Mary travel with three people?)*

Depending on which meaning is true, the list could be reworded, perhaps with a relative clause or an additional conjunction, or by re-ordering:

- Mary travelled to New York with Jim Smith and a doctor and a scholar.
- Mary travelled to New York with a scholar and Jim Smith, who was a doctor.
- Mary travelled to New York with a doctor, a scholar, and Jim Smith. *(with or without the serial comma)*

15.2.3 Direct Speech

Commas are used to separate narration from direct speech. A comma is used at the end of a quotation (inside the quotation marks) when describing narration follows the dialogue:

- "They will be here by five," said the secretary.

A comma may also be used at the end of a clause introducing a quote:

- The secretary said, "They will be here by five."

Narrative clauses may also be separated from direct speech with a comma when an action directly describes the quote, with verbs such as *to say, to ask*, and *to reply*:

- He handed her the envelope, saying, "Here's your letter."

The comma is <u>not</u> used when we use another form of punctuation to end the quotation, such as an exclamation mark or question mark:

- "Run!" she yelled.
- "Are you sure you know the way out?" the princess asked.

A full stop is used if the narrative text either side of the quote is not directly connected to the quote:

- "There's nowhere left to go." Resigned to his fate, Jim sat down.
- Jim was mad as he spoke into the phone. "Where are my eggs?"

Direct speech may be broken around narrative text. If the quotation is a continuing sentence divided by narrative, the narrative text may end with another comma. If the continuing quotation starts a new sentence, a full stop should be used:

- "Let's get you out of those wet clothes," she said, "and into something clean." *(The quote is one continuing sentence.)*
- "I'm not coming," he told her. "Nothing you can say will persuade me." *(The quote contains two separate sentences.)*

15.2.4 Separating Information

Additional information may be added to sentences separated by what can be called **parenthetical commas**. These behave the same way as parentheses. The information between two commas may be considered additional, and removing it should not affect the meaning of the sentence. Such information can be added for extra detail or commentary, and can come in the form of a few extra words or entire phrases or clauses:

- The dress was unsuitable.
- The dress, old and smelly, was unsuitable.
- The dress, would you believe, was unsuitable.
- The dress, old and smelly through years of use and no particular care for its upkeep, was unsuitable.

Parenthetical commas may also be used to move information from elsewhere in the sentence:

- Kylie prepared to watch the fireworks with great excitement.
- Kylie, with great excitement, prepared to watch the fireworks.
- Kylie prepared, with great excitement, to watch the fireworks.

If you don't put commas around such information, the sentence can become confusing:

- The dress of course was unsuitable. *(This makes the dress appear to belong to course, which does not work.)*
- Kylie with great excitement prepared to watch the fireworks. *(This makes the excitement sound like part of Kylie's name.)*

15.2.5 Adverbials

Commas often follow adverbs or adverbial phrases used at the start of a sentence. This is done in the same way as using a comma to separate a subordinate clause at the start of a sentence. These adverbials frame the sentence with information that would typically come later (such as time, manner, or a comment), placing information before the main clause:

- In time, we learnt the truth.
- Quick as a flash, she threw the flaming pan into the sink.
- Actually, there are no correct answers.

The comma comes directly after the adverb or complete adverbial phrase.

The adverb **however** is a well-known example of this, and is often taught as always being followed by a comma when placed at the start of a clause:

- However, the deal was not accepted.

This is only true when *however* is used to mean **on the other hand / in contrast** (as a linking adverb). But *however* may also be used to mean **by whatever means**, which does not use a comma. In the following example, *however* is part of an adverbial phrase, so the comma comes at the end of the phrase, not directly after the adverb:

- However much you want it, you cannot have my cake.

15.3 Ending Sentences

Most sentences end with a full stop, or period (.). This tells us the sentence is complete. Other options include exclamation marks (!) and question marks (?).

Exclamation marks can be used to add emphasis; demonstrating surprise, anger, and other emotions. They are particularly useful for exclamations in dialogue and for sharing surprising or alarming news:

- Oh my! *(exclamation)*
- "You're not coming with me!" *(dialogue)*
- The butcher has escaped – lock up your pigs! *(alarming news)*
- Sofa for sale – now 50% off! *(exciting news)*

Exclamation marks can be associated with lazy writing, when they are used instead of more effective language. However, as demonstrated in **14.1 Punctuation and Formatting**, they can alter the tone of a sentence when used correctly. In the example below, an exclamation mark sets a different tone:

- I won the prize, I'm so happy.
- I won the prize, I'm so happy!

Question marks are used at the end of sentences that ask questions. They can be added to grammatically formed questions (i.e. with inverted question form) or to statements presented as questions (tag questions):

- Where are the nuclear detonators? *(standard present simple question form)*
- I told you that? *(tag question)*

Tag questions are common in spoken English, and are useful when writing dialogue and informal correspondence, but for most contexts it is more appropriate to use the correct question form in writing:

- I told you that?
  → Did I tell you that?

Questions can also be ended with a full stop for **rhetorical questions**, where an answer is not expected. This helps demonstrate attitudes in writing:

- I packed another box pull of pens. This tiresome job never seemed to end. Where did my life go wrong.

An exclamation mark can be used for questions in situations where a dramatic emotion is more important than the question being asked; for example, when a question is expressed forcefully. This implies that the question is not being asked for an answer, but as an expression of emotion:

- "What have you done!"

Dramatic questions are sometimes punctuated with both a question mark and an exclamation mark. This is a matter of style and may not be considered acceptable in certain contexts, but a common technique is to combine the two punctuation marks in either order (?! or !?):

- "Where are you taking me?!"

In some situations, sentences are left open, for example when we use a colon (:) to open a list or a comma (,) to open a letter with salutations.

15.4 Semi-Colons

The semi-colon (;) is rather nuanced in use and as such not always properly understood or used, even by native speakers. It has practically the same effect as a conjunction, without adding a word. It is typically used to connect two related main clauses which would otherwise form two separate sentences (i.e. neither clause should be dependent or include connecting words):

- The kittens escaped; there was chaos in the shopping centre.
- I am so happy we hired her; the last cook was awful.

Semi-colons are useful for bringing clauses closer together, which can vary your flow and draw direct attention to a consequence:

- Fifteen per cent of employees were late last week; dismissals are to be announced shortly.

The above example could work as two sentences, but the semi-colon draws the dramatic second sentence closely to the cause. If you used a conjunction like *so* or *therefore*, the sentence would sound more reasoned (and reasonable) and lose some of the impact.

Semi-colons can also be used in lists, to separate items that already contain commas or to separate longer items (particularly if your list includes entire clauses):

> The following groups of people were given priority boarding: those who had booked two months in advance; those who booked the VIP package; families with young children; the elderly and the infirm.

15.5 Quotations

Quotes are usually demonstrated in English with quotation marks ("") around words, phrases, or sentences. There are various conventions for demonstrating quotations, however, depending on the style used. Apostrophes may be used instead of quotation marks, 'like this', and *italics* may be used when highlighting foreign or unfamiliar words.

Quotes may also be shown separated from the text, in block quotes:

> Block quotes might look like this. They may be formatted with various different styles to the main text.

Punctuation belonging to a quotation typically belongs inside quotation marks, while punctuation belonging to the surrounding sentence belongs outside the quotation marks. However, in American English, if the quotation ends a sentence the punctuation should be included in the quotation marks, whether it is a complete sentence or not. Here are a few examples:

- "This is an example of a complete sentence being quoted." It ends with a full stop.
- "This is an example of a complete sentence being quoted and framed by a narrative action," said the teacher. "It is connected to the framing sentence with a comma."
- A sentence quoting "only a few words or phrases" might look this, with no additional punctuation belonging to the quote.
- A British sentence ending in a quote of a few words or a phrase would look "like this". *(UK, full stop placed after closing quotation mark)*
- An American sentence ending in a quote of a few words or a phrase would look "like this." *(US, period placed before closing quotation mark)*

There are many additional ways of showing quotations. Pay attention to how other writers present their quotes, particularly if you are writing for a specific organisation or publication. Be aware, also, that some writers go against convention in ways that are difficult to imitate. The American novelist Cormac McCarthy, for example, does not use quotation marks at all (requiring a great deal of skill to indicate speech). Such exceptions require a mastery of the skill which may not always be clear for readers; other exceptions may, in fact, prove ineffective. The conventional methods are the most common because they work.

15.6 Capital Letters

In most texts, capital letters (letters in upper case) are used for the first letter of a sentence, for the first letter of a proper noun (or each important word of a proper noun phrase), for the pronoun "I" (and to spell out specific letters), and for certain acronyms and abbreviations:

- This sentence starts with a capital T and goes on to spell out a specific letter.
- The name and title of a Prime Minister (like Winston Churchill) start with capitals.
- Abbreviations such as IBM and GMC are written in capitals.

Pay particular attention to using capitals with proper nouns. You may cause confusion with inconsistent capitals when capitalised and non-capitalised nouns can refer to two different things. For example some buildings, such as pubs, may be named after animals, which would look strange if not properly capitalised:

- Jim and Wendy met in the dog and duck. *(animals?)*
- Jim and Wendy met in the Dog and Duck. *(more clearly a building)*

Capital letter use can depend on style. Key areas to look out for are place names, the names of institutions and organisations, dates, times, and compass directions. With all of these, a good general rule is that capitals are used when the noun specifically identifies the object, but not when the noun refers to the object as one of many possibilities:

- I studied at Nottingham University. *("University" used as part of the name)*
- My university was in Nottingham. *("university" not used as part of the name)*
- The River Nile is 4,160 miles long. *("River" used as part of the name)*
- The Nile is a very long river. *("river" not used as part of the name)*

- The West imposed sanctions on the East. *("West" and "East" refer to identifiable political regions)*
- We travelled west for two weeks. *("west" refers to a general direction)*

Capitals may be used more flexibly when a noun is used in an abstract or very specific situation, to highlight a particular convention or idea. This may highlight the difference between referring to an institution, e.g. *the Catholic Church,* or a location, e.g. *the Catholic church.* It may also highlight an importantly labelled object, for example:

- If you wish to apply for a Residence Visa, fill in the application.

As a general noun, "residence visa" does not need to be capitalised, but in the context of specific instructions relating to a specific visa process, it may be. Such use should be applied carefully and clearly. If you wish to highlight a particular object with capitals, it must be treated as a proper noun consistently.

Titles and other important sentences can be written in Title Case. Typically, titles only capitalise the first letter of the first word and all the important words. What is considered an important word varies, but it usually means leaving only articles, prepositions, and conjunctions in lower case. Longer prepositions and conjunctions (i.e. those with more than one syllable) may also appear in upper case:

- The President Shocks the World by Snoring Throughout Speech *("Throughout" remains capitalised as it is a longer preposition.)*

Sometimes, the first letter of every word in a title is capitalised (full title case), and sometimes only the first letter is capitalised, as with sentence case (more common for captions or subheadings).

As variations in Title Case may indicate, to be consistent and accurate with capitals it is important to refer to a style guide relevant to your context. Style guides should lay out conventions for all capital letter use and exceptions, and if you find a situation that a style guide does not cover then you may be able to logically compare it to other examples in the guide, or otherwise know to query it.

16. Numbers and Dates

Numbers may be shown in writing with numerals (1, 2, 3...) or written words (one, two, three...). This may be a matter of choice or a dictated style. Style guides often have clear guidelines for choosing when to write each, such as using full words for numbers ten and under, and numerals for numbers 11 and over. This is because written numbers can look more aesthetic within a text, but larger numbers take more time to read and numerals are immediately recognisable. Other common conventions include using numerals strictly for:

- units of measurement *(12 miles)*
- people's ages *(34 years old)*
- dates *(20th January)*

and using written words for:

- centuries *(nineteenth century)*
- approximations *(around eight thousand years ago)*

For money, a mixture of numerals (for most numbers) and words (for large round figures) are typically used *(£18, $25,432, £58 million)*.

Sometimes, only numerals or words may be used within a single sentence, so these conventions may be ignored for the sake of consistency within a particular sentence.

Usually, numbers are separated every three digits, but this can be done in one of three styles – with commas, spaces, or nothing:

- 1,000,000
- 1 000 000
- 100000

Hyphens are not typically used with written numbers except for adjective forms (e.g. *an 86-foot boat*) or if numbers higher than 11 are to be spelled out (e.g. *twenty-one*). Check style guides for these conventions.

Other number conventions may be flexible, but after you consider the different possibilities do use the same style throughout a document. Mixing styles is unlikely to cause too much confusion, but consistency aids clarity and professionalism. To illustrate a style consideration in action, the rest of this chapter focuses on dates, which are used by almost everyone.

16.1 Date Formats

Calendar dates can be written in a wide variety of ways in English, and may depend on how formal your writing is, your personal style, and whether you are writing in British or American English. In British English, dates are usually written in the order **day – month – year**, while in American English they are written **month – day – year**. Both of these styles have their uses: the British system goes from small to large units of time, while the American system makes it easier to collate data within monthly periods (for example, when ordering documents numerically dated by month and year).

The style you choose for writing the date depends on how formal you wish the document to be and how much space you have. The important detail is that you are accurate and consistent. Do not use different styles within the same document, unless you have a good reason.

In both British and American English, the date can be written in abbreviated forms, either as a group of numbers (separated by hyphens - , slashes / or periods .), or with the first few letters of the month.

16.1.1   British Abbreviated Dates

- 13/04/18, 13.04.18, 13-04-18
- 13/04/2018, 13.04.2018, 13-04-2018
- 13Apr2018, 13-Apr-18

16.1.2 American Abbreviated Dates

- 04/13/18, 04.13.18, 04-13-18
- 04/13/2018, 04.13.2018, 04-13-2018
- Apr. 13, 2018

In some circumstances, you may find the year comes before the month, then the day (a reverse of the standard British format). This is not common in English speaking countries, except in some technical texts.

16.1.3 Dates in British English

For British English dates, **day – month – year**, the 13th day of the month April, year 2018, might be written in this order of complexity:

- 13 April
- 13 April 2018
- 13th April 2018
- the 13th of April 2018
- the 13th of April, 2018

In the last two examples, **the** and **of** are optional, but if you do use them you should add both **the** and **of**. Avoid writing only *13th of April* or *the 13th April* (which could be taken to mean the 13th April month).

In British English, commas are not necessary, though they can be used to separate month and year as a matter of style.

The name of the day, when used, comes before the date, and should either be separated by a comma or joined by **the** and **of**:

- Sunday, 13 April, 2018
- Sunday the 13th of April, 2018

16.1.4 Dates in American English

In American English, the month comes before the day, which means you cannot use **of**, and ordinal numbers *(1st, 2nd, 3rd, 4th, etc.)* are rarely used. Commas should be used to separate the day and year, and the name of the day should come at the beginning. The date should therefore be written:

- April 13
- April 13, 2018
- Sunday, April 13, 2018

April the 13th or *April 13th* are not incorrect, but are uncommon, and may be considered mistakes amongst some speakers of American English.

16.1.5 Choosing the Right Date Format

As English spreads internationally through email and the internet, the barriers between US and UK English lessen. You may also find more regional variations as, for example, Canadian English and Australian English respectively use the US and UK formats with more flexibility. Indeed, writers may generally be more flexible than in the past. For example, as a British writer raised using the British format, I also use the American order of **month – day – year** within spreadsheets and when naming documents, because I have found it is more effective for numerical sorting.

Many people aren't really aware of, or bothered by, whether a style is technically American or British English; it is more a case of understanding your audience to know what is expected. If a particular format is expected, it would be inadvisable to use a different style. In this case, however, you can at least use the regional understanding as a starting point to decide on a style.

17. Bolder Writing

The earlier chapters of this book should help improve the overall quality of your writing, resulting in clear, respectable writing. Often, all that is required for writing to make an excellent impression is for it to be efficient and accurate. However, there may also be situations where you want your writing to stand out. If you want to write especially descriptively, or persuasively, you can employ more nuanced language, such as idiomatic language, superlative language, techniques like similes and metaphors, and unusual words and phrases. The challenge is not merely learning these new techniques, but using them effectively.

Remember, your writing is often most effective when it is selective rather than excessive. It should be understated rather than overstated. Consider the use of hyperbole (extreme, often unrealistic language):

- I'm so tired I could sleep for a year.
- I'm so hungry I could eat a horse.
- This product will change your life!

Hyperbole can be entertaining and engaging, but it is only appropriate in very particular circumstances. As a starting point, such extreme examples may be considered informal, and the nature of them being entertaining means they would be inappropriate for more serious subjects. Equally important, such examples needs to be very imaginative to be convincing, as creative language like this can often sound (ironically) very clichéd.

A **cliché** can refer to any word or phrase that has become overused. Clichés can sound effective (they become clichés because they are popular, after all), but they are unimaginative. Because they are common, clichés are seldom memorable or convincing. When your first instinct is to use clichéd language, ask how you might make it more interesting (see overleaf):

- He looked as happy as the cat that got the cream. *(cliché)*
- He looked as happy as the cat that discovered tin openers. *(a twist on the theme)*

This can be applied generally, to all the creative writing techniques you may be tempted to use. To be creative, you must search for words, phrases, and ideas that are not commonly used. But **only** do this only when you want to draw particular attention to something.

To return to the example of colours (see **2.1 Why Complicate Life?**), describing something with a very specific and accurate colour only works if the rest of your writing is clear and simple. If you use lots of advanced language, that exceptional colour would become another in a chain of distracting terms.

When attempting to add more interesting language to your writing, also be aware of how it will be read. Context can create restrictions. Unusual language in formal writing may seem confusing or less reliable. Describing a product in unrealistic, but entertaining, terms may be useful in some circumstances and damaging in another. Consider the following example:

- Every bottle of beer contains a thousand bubbles of happiness.

This creative phrase could help the product sound fun, and not to be taken too seriously. It might be appropriate for a light-hearted party-going audience, but inappropriate for someone who prefers respectable, complex drinks. For another example, concluding a business report with enthusiastic language such as *"The results were amazing, and should be acted on in a flash."* targets the wrong audience. Reports are not necessarily read for entertainment, and such language might be deemed untrustworthy or unprofessional. In academic and business writing, this is crucially important. For the same reason that passive, objective statements are useful, it is best to avoid anything too creative, in order to be taken seriously.

What if you are specifically writing creative prose? Even here – for example, in writing fiction – you must be careful to set the right tone. When using a colourful narrator, and writing in the first person, you can include creative language as fits the character, but otherwise the purpose of your writing is still to make your ideas clear and easy to read. Anything that draws attention to the writing itself doesn't work well. People do not read fiction, after all, to see what creative language you can use; they read it for a good story. Creative writing can work in specific circumstances, such as when including surprising language in humour or gruesome details in horror, but mostly you should choose the language that best moves the narrative forwards. Consider the following examples, if used in a thriller:

- He sprinted down the alley, scattering bins with his free hand to trip up his pursuer.
- He sprinted down the alley, scattering bins with the clatter of a collapsing scaffold, hoping to trip up his pursuer.

Creative as the second example is, it is too cumbersome for a fast chase, and will create a different (and confusing) image in the mind of a reader.

Again, this is a principle to apply generally. Whichever creative techniques you employ, they all share a similar impact, creating a break from the expected, simple writing. Always think about who will read your text and how they will experience it. If you want to make your writing bolder, consider not just how effectively a technique captures your idea, but how it will impact the flow, tone, and credibility of your text.

Also remember that being bold with your writing does not always mean making it complicated, or colourful, or unique. Writing can stand out by being incredibly easy to follow, too.

17.1 Becoming More Engaging

Clear writing with rare, strategic variations may keep a reader engaged on its own. If you specifically want to draw certain emotions from a reader, however, there are a few additional techniques that might help. The theory of writing in the second person is covered in **10.2 Second Person**. Also consider the difference it makes to use active sentences, as covered in **12. Passive and Active Writing**. Both of these techniques can make writing more engaging:

- Every new parent will love this pram.
  → You will love this pram.
- The cinema is being closed down.
  → The Council are closing down the cinema.

Both of these examples work on the same principle: they move from the general to the specific. By clearly defining the actor, a clearer picture is created, drawing the reader in. Specific images are very important to take a reader from reading for information to actively picturing a situation. This is relevant in all fields of writing. Sentences with more direct agency can make even detached writing more engaging. In the following example, the second sentence is actually longer, but it is clearer because it is more active:

- Proof theory is where proofs are represented as formal mathematical objects.
  → Proof theory is a branch of logic that represents proofs as formal mathematical objects.

Another way to engage the reader is to ask questions. This is commonly done in advertising and headlines:

- Most carpet cleaners can't remove stubborn stains.
  → Can your carpet cleaner remove stubborn stains?
- A new study has proposed the existence of mice on the moon.
  → Are mice really living on the moon?

Questions appeal to readers' curiosity and draw them personally into the text. Often the brain has a need to read on to find the answer. The same effect can be produced by leaving out information, or hinting at something still to come. This is often employed at the end of sections of a creative text, such as chapter endings, with what is commonly called a **cliff-hanger**, finishing with an unresolved situation:

> Harold held on tight, his legs hanging over the edge of the cliff, the drop impossibly far down. If he reached across to the tree roots, he might lose his grip. But there was no other option, and he was getting weaker by the moment. He went for it.

Ending a scene here would create a literal cliff-hanger, encouraging the reader to keep going to find out what happens next.

Inspiring curiosity has become particularly common in online headlines and email subjects, designed to make people click them. These often open questions or make bold statements that demand more information:

- Can you afford not to follow these tips?
- You'll never guess which celebrity survives only on burgers!

These techniques must be used sparingly to be effective. Titles like these, in fact, are disparagingly referred to as **clickbait**, and may encourage resentment as readers feel manipulated. Employing such techniques takes delicate care, and again works best when the rest of your text is respectable and clear.

To be safe, the best way to engage a reader will always be to produce writing that is easy to read and understand: writing that focuses on the important details, without providing redundant or distracting language. Only slight variations are needed to make things stand out. The final and perhaps most important tip in writing to engage, therefore, is simply **don't try too hard**. It shows.

18. Offensive Language

The English-speaking world has a colourful history, which sadly includes a great deal of imperial, gendered, and national hierarchies (to name a few). As well as creating a flexible and diverse language, this has also created a language littered with negative terms and phrases, many of which may not be immediately obvious. Offensive language is therefore a very important area to consider, and you should develop an awareness for how particular words and phrases may be interpreted.

In business writing and other formal writing, including academic writing and formal correspondence, the slightest hint of offensive language can undermine your entire text. You may be tempted to use it in less formal settings, however, and in fiction in particular, to create a certain atmosphere or to add realism. Always consider the tastes of your audience. Just because such language is possible does not mean it is necessary.

This chapter looks at some of the specific areas of language that can be considered offensive, so that you can consider the impact they may have on your readers.

18.1 Swear Words

Swear words, or curse words, are a collection of exclamations used for the purpose of offending, or for expressing extreme emotion. Many of them have explainable meanings, often to do with waste, genitalia, or religion. Such words may occur in writing when quoting speech or thoughts, but should seldom be found in descriptive writing. When writing, you have time to consider your points carefully, and there is almost always a better way to make a point than to use a swear word. Removing swear words, for example in a piece of writing where you are expressing your frustration, gives your writing more authority and can make your message clearer.

Another consideration with swear words is that many people see them as lazy and unimaginative. There are times when expressing extreme emotion is

124

precisely your goal, but even in these cases there are more effective techniques than interjecting a swear word. Another, more specific, adjective may add a greater level of persuasion, for example.

Be aware, also, of how different words carry different strengths. The perception of swear words in English regularly changes. Hundreds of years ago, some of our more offensive swear words were considered normal parts of speech, whilst in the last few generations the strength of other swear words has greatly declined.

The strength of swear words may also be regional: a particular word may be considered less offensive, for example, in regions where it is not commonly used or understood, and conversely more offensive where it is.

The most acceptable occasion for swearing in writing, if there is one, is when writing in character, such as through dialogue or creative first person writing. Even in these circumstances, however, it is important to consider how frequently and strongly such language is used. As with other techniques, overuse loses impact, and in this case could actively put readers off.

18.2 Gendered Language

In the English language, gender roles are mainly assigned to living creatures. This means that gender in English typically relates directly to sex, as opposed to linguistic functions, which creates a political consideration, as patriarchal (i.e. male-dominated) societies have left a mark in the way English is used. Many words, phrases, and conventions that were traditionally accepted may now be deemed offensive.

An example of this is covered in **13.3 Salutations and Valedictions**, with the variations of greetings for men and women. The titles *Mrs* and *Miss* may be considered sexist as they define a woman by her marital status (with or without a man), whilst *Mr* does not define a man by any relationship. *Ms* is therefore a more neutral title to use. There are many less obvious, but similarly weighted, language conventions to look out for.

It was once common to refer to an unknown person in the masculine; for example, starting a letter *Dear **Sir*** or writing *Someone was here – whoever **he** was left a trail of mud.* This might be done unintentionally, but as well as being potentially offensive it can also cause problems in understanding. A better option is to use ungendered language with unknown subjects, which can be done with *he or she, Sir or Madam,* and in the plural *they / them.*

To ensure you do not cause offence with gendered language, look out for anything that refers to one sex alone, without reason, and consider carefully any words or phrases that refer to *man, woman,* or gendered nouns. It is not always possible to avoid using a single gender, and writers can choose one gender or another to refer to a general subject, but you should be aware of it and address the issue when possible. One solution, for example, is to alternate between genders for an unknown subject, for example referring to *he* in one instance and *she* in another. This may be a matter of style, and specific to a text, but the important thing is to make such decisions with care.

Also consider any language that suggests a gender bias. There are a great many gender stereotypes out there which should be avoided. Sexuality is a similarly delicate area in language, as it has been used to provoke and cause insults. Avoid any language that refers to gender or sexuality in a negative light, which includes using words as slurs.

18.3 Racial Slurs

While general swear words are offensive by convention, racial slurs carry the added weight of historical conflict and oppression, making them more offensive to specific cultures. A difficulty with racial slurs in English is that many speakers perceive them lightly because they do not perceive them from the culture's point of view. Certain terms may be considered less offensive by the speaker, either because the impact has faded with the history of such words, or because the slur does not apply to the person that uses it. To someone on the receiving end of such slurs, however, the interpretation can be incredibly different, so take care to understand and avoid such words.

There are many obvious racial slurs in English, with slang terms that define people as a particular race, nationality, or culture. These should be identifiable by their use. Other terms may be less obviously offensive, such as the words used to refer to people by the colour of their skin. If you must use a label for ethnic groups, you may consider consulting a reference book or website which clearly labels words as offensive or taboo, such as the *Oxford Advanced Learner's Dictionary.* Otherwise, look for advice from someone of that group. There are words used in English for ethnicity that may appear innocent but are not. Many are considered offensive simply due to their suggestion of otherness.

It is also important to look out for words and phrases that may not obviously carry a racial meaning. When using any word or phrase that refers to a group of people, particularly if it reflects colour or nationality, be sure to check its origins. In this area, the most immediate or obvious choice of word is not always the best one.

18.4 Disabilities and More

Language that refers to disabilities or other special circumstances that single people out can be seen in the same light as racial slurs and gendered language. This area is perhaps harder to spot, as **ableist language** (as it is known) is not always understood as such by people with no direct experience of disabilities. Words that refer to people with disabilities and mental health problems have entered the English language as everyday offences that are rarely considered as serious as swear words and racial slurs. Such language is no less offensive to certain people, however. Watch out for any words that refer to lack of intelligence, mobility, sanity, or other generalisations, and consider the origins of other, unclear negative words. Many of them come from insulting people based on real conditions, and should be avoided.

19. Editing

Writing is often considered the most difficult of the four key skills in English (compared to reading, speaking, and listening) because it demands the most precise use of language. This is because writing can be edited, and you do not need to commit to the first thing you produce. To be precise, **good writing requires editing**. Many writers have said there is no good writing, only rewriting (attributed variously to Robert Graves and Louis Brandeis). Indeed, you cannot apply all of the advice of this book, amongst other writing advice, during the act of writing itself. To put everything into practice, **you must edit** your text. The more time you can spend editing and rewriting, the better your writing will be.

Editing is not just about finding technical mistakes such as spelling errors. It is when you can make your writing as clear and effective as possible. It is a skill in itself, requiring as much practice as the act of writing. Note, though, that it is incredibly difficult for any writer to flawlessly edit their own work. With your own writing, you already understand what you want to say, so you cannot read it fresh, and are likely to miss errors. Edit your text to the best of your ability, but also seek a second opinion.

Where do you begin with editing? In professional editing, there are **seven Cs** to look out for. Ask yourself if your writing is:

- Clear
- Concise
- Consistent
- Correct
- Coherent
- Complete
- Credible

You can start by rereading your work with three key goals in mind. Cover all these points by aiming for **clarity**, **correctness**, and **consistency**. If your writing is clear, correct, and consistent, it should also be concise, coherent, credible, and complete.

19.1 Clarity

Using simple writing with common terms and structures to present ideas is the easiest way to ensure your writing is clear. This includes using conventional systems of structure and paragraphing, and the most direct grammar (such as using the active voice instead of the passive). When you are editing your work, you can look out for all these ideas by hunting for unnecessary words and complex language or structures.

Unnecessary words include any word that does not add essential information to a sentence. These can be ineffective details or filler words, words which slip into writing in the same way as they do in speech. Common examples of filler words include the adverbs *just* and *really*, which often add little additional meaning. You may also find unnecessary prepositions and prepositional phrases, such as prepositions added to directions (*climbed **up** onto*) or dialogue (*shouted **out***). Often we add such fillers out of habit rather than because they are needed. Identify these words by searching for adverbs, adjectives, and prepositions. Remember George Orwell's tip: *If it is possible to cut a word out, always cut it out.* (*Politics and the English Language*, 1946) Cutting out words both shortens and clarifies your writing.

Complex language and structures require a more careful eye, due to their specific uses, as discussed in **2.1 Why Complicate Life?** and **7.2 Specialist Vocabulary**. Always ask if a complex word or structure is necessary, and consider **why** it is necessary. If you can't answer why, then it is probably not needed. Even when it is needed, look for the simplest and clearest way to present it. This can be as simple as explaining a word when it is first used, or rearranging a structure that has become unclear:

- The astrobleme was being studied by three different departments.
  → The astrobleme, a crater caused by a meteorite, was being studied by three different departments.
- All books that were checked out by the captain of the chess club were stained by chocolate when they were returned by him.
  → All the books the captain of the chess club checked out were stained by chocolate when he returned them.

129

Exactly how you can identify and change such language will depend on the text itself. Pay attention to how your sentence components connect to each other. Is the subject of each verb clear? Is each prepositional phrase clearly connected to one object? Is it clear who or what your pronouns refer to? This may sound like a lot to consider, but bear in mind it is only in your complicated and longer sentences that these issues become problems. Confusion occurs in sentences with multiple verbs, sentences with multiple actors, and longer sentences in general, particularly those involving lots of additional information. These are the sentences to study carefully.

When using multiple verbs in a sentence, be careful that a confusing additional actor does not come between the subject and the verb. In such cases it may be easiest to restate the subject:

- I went to the shop, where Jim worked, and met Carla.
- I went to the shop, where Jim worked, and I met Carla.

This is a deliberately subtle example. The commas fairly clearly separate *where Jim worked* from the rest of the sentence, but restating the subject helps avoid potential confusion. In other situations, with another actor, it could become unclear which actor the additional information refers to, particularly when dealing with prepositional phrases and clauses connected with ambiguous pronouns:

- An inconsistency was found in the report, which we needed to discuss. *(Do we need to discuss the inconsistency or the report?)*
- They opened the door with a metal bar. *(Does the metal bar describe the door or the tool used to open it?)*

These problems can be resolved in a number of ways depending on the text. Sometimes the context might make the meaning clear: if we know a character is searching for a way to open the door beforehand, we might understand the metal bar to be a tool. When there is a danger of ambiguity, make efforts to clarify such connections. For example, a verb might define the relationship better than a preposition:

- They opened the door **using** a metal bar.

In other cases, it may be necessary to elaborate. Longer sentences are sometimes needed to add clarity. Considering our other example, explicitly describing what is discussed works better than using a pronoun:

- An inconsistency was found in the report, **so** we needed to discuss **a revision**.

This makes the relationships within the sentence clearer, even though the sentence becomes longer.

With longer sentences, also pay attention to lists, to ensure that all the actors of verbs are clear, and that the correct number of words are present. A common mistake in lists is not attributing conjunctions correctly:

- We wanted a new chair, a desk, a computer with a mouse and a keyboard.

In the above sentence, the main list should be three items, *a new chair, a desk,* **and** *a computer with a mouse and a keyboard.* There is a missing conjunction. The meaning may still be clear, but it is technically incorrect and it could be argued that the keyboard is unrelated to the computer. In situations where the nouns are closely related and their attribution is important, this error could lead to a lot of confusion:

- The visiting team includes a business analyst with an intern, a sales manager with a personal assistant and a secretary.
- The visiting team includes a business analyst with an intern, and a sales manager with a personal assistant and a secretary.

In this example, the list could include three items (a business analyst +1, a sales manager +1 and a secretary) or two items (a business analyst +1 and a sales manager +2), depending on the additional conjunction. In a context where such information was used, for example, to buy travel tickets, the ambiguous list could lead to a purchasing mistake.

These are only starting points to look out for in editing for clarity. Spotting unclear language takes practice and a strong understanding of the building blocks of English, in order to keep an eye on the relationships between different components within sentences. These basic principles, however, should help you develop an attitude to seek clarity in your writing.

19.2 Correctness

Being correct in your writing means using accurate language. This requires correct punctuation, correct spelling, and correct words and structures, as well as correct (or at least correctly connected) ideas. Accuracy is more important in writing than any other language skill, as mistakes in writing can look unprofessional or unprepared, and do not benefit from the social cues that make spoken mistakes easier to interpret. There is also less excuse for inaccurate writing, as it can be revised and plenty of tools exist to help improve your language.

Punctuation and spelling can be studied and learnt as a discipline, and computer software provides a lot of help in this area. If you have a spell-check available, use it strategically and pay attention to your mistakes so that you learn from them. Computer spell-checks cannot spot everything (for example, consider homonyms with different spellings but the same sound), so be sure to re-read your writing thoroughly and check all the punctuation and spelling yourself. Take the time to look up words you are unsure of.

Editing in such a way, and committing to such editing, frees you up to write more fluently. Many students avoid writing practice because it can be time-consuming, and searching for the right words and spellings interrupts their flow. If this is the case for you, write to complete your ideas and edit the language afterwards. Various analogies exist for the process of writing that compare the first draft to generating material that you can later shape. There is no need to expect any writing to be perfect on a first attempt. When you have words on the page, it is easier to rearrange and improve them than if you have no words at all.

Correctness may depend on purpose. The internet contains many lists of "common mistakes" and "words that don't mean what you think they mean" in English. In some cases these are useful, but in others they refer to archaic or stylistically specific uses. Being accurate and technically correct is not always as simple as following reference books. English is based on patterns, not rules, and language use and vocabulary is constantly evolving. Common usage of any grammatical structure or vocabulary creates patterns that are popularly understood.

When editing for accuracy, your understanding of English in practical use becomes very important. For example, the word *decimate* was originally taken from the Romans to mean *kill one in ten*, but in modern use it is used to mean *destroy*. The original use is very rare, and unlikely to be understood without a clear context. With such a word, the meaning which is more common and generally understood (i.e. the modern use) is more correct. Conversely, in specific niches you may find names and titles (for example, scientific theories) that do not follow typical naming or grammatical conventions. In such cases, if everyone writing in that niche uses an unusual form of a title, and it is that audience you are writing for, the unusual form would be more correct.

Language rules attempt to record, and share, the patterns that emerge, but they do not dictate them. The way we use English develops based on people's practical use rather than by following books. With this in mind, refer to the most respected (and up to date) reference books for advice, and be wary of discussions surrounding these books, particularly for newer language or words in transition.

The rules of the English language are useful because they help avoid confusion and prevent misunderstandings. This is the first and most important reason to be correct in your English: to make sure what you're saying makes sense (and says *what you want to say*). A misspelled word, a misplaced comma, an inappropriate adjective, or inaccurate use of tenses can all confuse or change the meaning of a sentence. So remember, throughout editing, that the purpose of editing for accuracy is to be clearly understood, not merely to satisfy the rules.

So how do you ensure accurateness? First, make it a personal quest to challenge everything. This will give you an appreciation for the most important rules and why they matter. The following example shows a misuse of punctuation:

- The man growled, "You're finished in this town".

While the meaning in this example is clear, the misplaced full stop/period takes the reader out of the moment, drawing attention to the writing and its inaccuracy. This is a big mistake if you are telling a story, not because it affects understanding, but because it affects the reading experience. Even a small mistake like this can thus have a recognisable negative result.

Some areas of writing are more ambiguous. With punctuation, you may find debate when dealing with commas and conjunctions. For example, there is debate surrounding serial commas (covered in **15.2.2 Lists and the Serial Comma**), and there is not always a right answer for the best way to use it. However, while the best choice may be debatable, there are almost always *wrong* choices, which reduce clarity. In cases where you have more flexible options, questioning whether or not your decision affects the clarity can help answer which choice (if any) is correct.

Identifying wrong choices helps you to recognise why the rules matter:

- I have visited ten countries.
- I visited ten countries.

In this example, the choice of tense is important, as without more context the past simple statement sounds incomplete. When we talk about built experience, such as locations we have been to, the present perfect effectively tells us **up to now**, while the past simple suggests this experience was completed **in the past,** and so invites the question *when?* However, if your sentence goes on to answer that question, the past simple tense is correct:

- I visited ten countries in my twenties.
- I visited ten countries on a business trip.

Consider another example:

- I won't have cereal as I have already eaten breakfast.
- I won't have cereal as I already ate breakfast.

Here, the present perfect is technically more accurate, linking the past action to the present condition, but it is not entirely necessary as the past simple, telling us the action was completed in the recent past, conveys a very similar message (particularly brought closer in meaning by *already*). There is a technical difference in grammar, but both options are likely to be understood the same way by a reader. Such concerns necessarily relate to context. In some contexts, two words may similarly be used interchangeably while in different contexts they could highlight an important difference, as covered in **2.1 Why Complicate Life?**

There are also cases when rules are debated with little real purpose. The argument over **split infinitives** (placing an adverb between a verb and its particle) is a case in point. This was done in the original *Star Trek* franchise, where the character Captain Kirk determined "**to boldly go** where no man has gone before", with *boldly* separating *to* and *go*. This emphasises how the action is done. However, some argue that split infinitives should be avoided. It does not appear to affect the meaning (no one would interpret *to go boldly*, *boldly to go*, or *to boldly go* differently), so why does the rule exist?

Answering **why** shows how important accuracy is. In the case of the tense choices, when we ask why *I have visited* is important, it is because *I visited* refers to a specific time and will sound incomplete without the reader knowing what that time period was. In the case of the split infinitive, there appears to be little difference in meaning. So why does it matter? You can find out by looking at where the rule comes from. This information is often available online, for instance through websites like Wikipedia. Using the link in the **Recommended Reading** list, you can find the split infinitive was first identified as disagreeable in the nineteenth century. In 1834, an anonymous passage in American literature presented a rule that the participle and verb "must not be separated". Certain grammarians followed with explanations that the split infinitive was a "disagreeable affection", "a common fault", and "flying in the face of common usage". According to those writers, the split infinitive is inaccurate because it is different or does not look elegant. These are bad reasons for restricting your use of language.

When doing such research, do check the sources, though; Wikipedia typically has citations to help you verify information. Also consider wider reading in such areas. There are many excellent books exploring language history, including Bill Bryson's *The Mother Tongue* (1990). Continually hunting for answers **why** will not only help you identify when your writing needs improving, it will help you remember and apply the important rules in the future. You can also decide which rules are less important.

A final point to recognise is that no one can reach a level of perfect accuracy alone. Your ultimate purpose should be to be understood, and you cannot truly tell if your writing will be properly understood until you share it. In some contexts this is less important than in others. For example, in email correspondence, personal practice and first drafts, you do not need every detail to be perfect, but for more serious writing, do not be afraid to ask for help. In fact, expect to need help. Even a native English speaker must edit and rewrite, and have others check their writing, before it can be accurate. I have been writing all my life, and I need at least two or three rounds of editing with other people before I can confidently publish anything without errors (if then!).

19.3 Consistency

Consistency is essential in writing for three reasons:

1. To ensure your writing does not contradict itself.
2. To avoid confusing variations.
3. To logically apply your chosen style.

The first two points are hopefully clear: if your writing contains variations and inconsistencies, it can weaken arguments and trip up or confuse readers. Inconsistent details show a lack of understanding, while inconsistent spelling, for example, might suggest two different ideas. Look out for consistency with any ideas or conventions that are repeated, whether it is the spelling of uncommon words, particular punctuation conventions, or something more specific like repeated facts or figures.

The third point is particular to the choices in English that are debatable. Even when a certain matter of style is not expected, if it is used logically and consistently, it will be seen as a **style choice** rather than a mistake. Inconsistent or illogical styles, on the other hand, are clear mistakes. You may, for example, write a text with British English spellings because you are most familiar with British English. This is a logical reason to apply a particular style, and it will inform consistent spelling. If you wrote the same text with a mixture of British and American spellings, however, it would be full of errors, as you have not logically applied one or the other style.

When editing, it is therefore essential that you look out for any areas of English that are flexible, and consider whether or not you have used them the same way throughout your text. A sensible way to do this is to keep track of your decisions in a separate document, such as a style sheet. You can list grammar, punctuation, and spelling decisions there, to refer back to and to help justify your choices.

20. Practice

Understanding the theory of writing will not improve your writing on its own. The only way to master any skill is to practise it as often as possible, and to learn from your experiences (good and bad). Write frequently and, equally important, edit carefully. Ask for feedback from people with enough knowledge to provide **constructive criticism** (that is, corrections that can help you improve). If you don't know anyone who can help, don't be afraid to search online. There are many writers' groups available where writers are keen to help each other improve in the craft.

There are many different ways to practise, and it is up to you to choose a way that suits your needs. Whatever you choose, remember that the more you write, and the more different styles you try, the quicker you will progress. Some ideas for practice in everyday life include:

- Develop written relationships with people, consistently emailing or sharing letters.
- Write stories based on your real-life experiences, like a diary.
- Write a blog, sharing it online and asking for reader feedback.
- Take notes, whenever possible, such as when in lectures, watching TV, or reading.
- Write reports on things you have seen or done, such as book or TV reviews.

Share your writing. Ask people to correct it. If your writing is part of your profession, consider hiring a proofreader or an editor. It is not enough to simply write, you must write with feedback. This is especially important in the workplace or when writing anything due for publication, and it applies to all English speakers, not just foreign learners. I miss mistakes in my own work, but thanks to working with editors I can identify these mistakes and eliminate them in the future. Unless someone else points out your mistakes, you will continue to make them.

There are teachers and trainers who encourage setting word counts or other challenges to ensure that you write a certain amount every day. This discipline may work for you, but I do not use it personally. I do believe in writing as much as possible, but, in my opinion, writing for the sake of hitting a number focuses on the wrong goal. If you do find daily targets helpful, remember that you are writing to improve and to learn. Writing a 100-word email that is sent and read, after all, may prove more educational than writing a 1,000-word essay that you keep to yourself.

Find what motivates you best. Practise in a way that works for you. Write things that you enjoy, and things that feel natural. Write things that are unusual and challenging, too, and always try to learn from it. If your writing is mostly focused on academic or business texts, try something creative. If you mostly write creatively, try something educational.

Bear in mind that practising writing by actually writing is only half of the challenge. Your writing will always be limited by your exposure to the writing of others. Until you see different conventions in use, you will not know how to use them. If you really want to improve your writing, **read more**. Read as much as possible, from as many different areas as possible. The more you read, the more you will understand, and the easier writing will become. As the blunt but accurate American writer Harlan Ellison said, "A writer who writes more than he reads is an amateur." As with writing, read thoughtfully and read with a critical eye. Question how different conventions work, look up new words, and ask if what you are reading is actually correct.

20.1 Tips for Faster Writing

A big barrier to practising writing may be the concern that it takes a long time. When you are trying to improve, it can be very time consuming thinking of the right words and phrases. This is something that comes with practice, and the more you write the quicker you will become. But what if you have a limited amount of time?

Preparation fosters faster writing. If you plan your topic and structure, and have an idea of what you want to convey, you can mentally start thinking of words and phrases to use before you get to writing them. It can be useful to brainstorm in this stage, simply noting words and phrases you want to use, not complete sentences.

When you start writing, try not to over-think it. It is easier to come back and correct mistakes than it is to continually stop and start. Writing with a sense of flow and fluency comes from relaxing. Don't worry about the result at first, just try to feel the words.

Setting a time limit can help, as necessity and urgency are great ways to encourage yourself. If you force yourself to complete a piece of writing in a set time, you have no option but to speed up, ignoring mistakes and not over-thinking. Connected to this, you may also want to set word count targets for a specific amount of time, with the aim to simply create sentences quickly. As stated above, though, be aware of limiting yourself with targets. Remember the targets are not the goal, they are tools to encourage writing.

Always re-read and edit your work to improve your speed. Noting the things you have done right will build confidence, while analysing your mistakes will help you avoid them in future.

Above all, remember that writing is a skill. It is not a piece of knowledge that can be learnt theoretically. Like a muscle, you must use the skill again and again for it to improve, and the more you use it the stronger it will get. If you want to write faster, you must write more.

20.2 Bending the Rules

As your skills in writing English improve, you will be increasingly faced with the temptation (and the need) to bend the rules of the language. A great many rules in English may be dictated by style guides, such as for punctuation and naming conventions, but there is a huge amount of English that sticks to unwritten, or at least arguable, rules. These uses are too diverse and nuanced to teach simply.

You can develop an understanding for them through extensive exposure to English in use, such as through reading and listening practice. Colloquial or other adaptive uses of English can be very specific, so if in doubt, consult with an English speaker who can tell you if you are using the language correctly. Particular areas to look out for include phrasal verbs, idiomatic words or phrases, and regional language.

Flexible English rules tend to be most useful in informal writing. It is rare that you will bend the rules in formal writing, where the most correct or conventional forms will be expected. However, you may see many variations in formal writing that don't necessarily bend rules so much as apply less common or more advanced rules. As with the general tips for writing practice, when it comes to bending the rules, you will only learn through extensive writing and reading of your own. Much of the nuance of English cannot easily be taught, only observed and applied.

Part 2

Practical Areas of Writing

How to Use This Section

Part 1 covered many general principles in English writing, all of which may be important in different writing contexts. Some of the considerations made in Part 1 refer to specific areas of writing, such as non-fiction, business writing, or creative writing, but could be applied differently in different areas. Looking at conventions for writing in context, you can find ideas to help write for specific purposes, so Part 2 offers tips that relate directly to context.

This section is only an introduction to the different ways English writing is adapted for different uses. It contains initial ideas for tackling these texts, with examples. Each of these topics could potentially be discussed in great detail, and require years of additional training to really perfect. If you have a particular interest in one area, look for other books and training on the specific topics. Every topic in this section has a wide range of literature surrounding it, and my intention here is only to begin bridging the tips of Part 1 to practical usage.

21. Academic Writing

Writing for academia, such as in publications, exams, and reports, is typically formal, descriptive, and direct. In general, academic writing should be straightforward, without creative use of English and without much bending of the rules, to give the clearest and simplest descriptions of processes, concepts, and discussions. Academic writing can be more complex than other forms of writing, however, in the overall structuring of ideas and the use of specialist language.

The structure of any non-fiction text should be planned to present points in a logical manner. In simple terms, for example, it makes sense to follow the chronological order of a process, or to group the points of an argument thematically. It is important to devise a structure to suit your purpose, as it will guide your writing and can help make your point effectively. In longer texts, this may include planning sections, chapters, and sub-headings before you begin writing.

Use of specialist language in academic writing depends strongly on your context (as discussed in **7.2 Specialist Vocabulary**). If you require specific vocabulary to discuss specialist topics, be aware that it may differ from common usage. Certain scientific theories, for example, may have names that dictate whether or not to use a definite article with them. Read widely to see how such language works within your field, and do not be afraid to challenge regular English usage if you are familiar with specialist language usage.

When writing for an academic niche, also use your wider reading to get an idea of the vocabulary that is commonly used and understood, and the terms that might need explaining. If you are concerned about whether or not a particular piece of vocabulary will be understood, include a brief explanation the first time you use a word, and again if there is a large break between usage. Otherwise, it may be sensible to compile a Glossary, indexing unusual words, at the end of your work.

Referencing is more important in academic writing than in other fields. There are many different conventions for referencing sources in English, which can depend on a specific publication or institution's style. These styles can dictate the use of footnotes and endnotes, and may contain precise requirements for references (such as using periods and commas around names, and deciding the order that the book's title and author's name are written in). Learn the particular reference system required for your writing, and be consistent with it, as errors here may be considered mistakes and reduce the credibility of your work.

Academic writing is generally formal and often impersonal. It is rare to discuss academic topics in the first person, or to reference actors involved when discussing general patterns, processes, or findings. It is therefore common to use the passive voice in academic writing:

- We studied the monkeys and found no signs of disease.
  (active, personal)
- The monkeys were studied and no signs of disease were found.
  (passive, impersonal)

Using the passive voice can lead to longer, indirect sentences. This is not a problem if it is the clearest and most neutral way to present your case. However, there are ways to keep such formal writing direct and simple. One method is to use an adjective formed from a verb (e.g. *studied monkeys*) together with a demonstrative verb (e.g. *show, prove, demonstrate*) to describe results:

- The studied monkeys showed no signs of disease.

Actors are needed in academic writing when you wish to discuss specific people's activities; for example, when discussing other writing and studies. In such cases, people are often referred to by surnames, or by their full names:

- Pavlov's experiments are still talked about today.
- The oldest person to be appointed first-time Prime Minister in Britain was Henry John Temple, 3rd Viscount Palmerston.

Beyond these starting points, the way that you structure and style your academic writing will need to be informed by your field, and may depend on the purpose of your writing. Academic writing can, for example, be used to inform or to argue, so while it should be neutral in style it may still require persuasive language. Even in the case of writing that must persuade or debate, bear in mind that neutral language is more likely to be taken seriously. Emotional or overly expressive language can undermine academic writing, as it draws attention to the writer, rather than the topic of discussion.

22. Profiles

Author profiles are necessary when you need to introduce yourself in publishing (such as for an article byline or a publishing credit), and are now almost essential when you write online. Even if your writing is limited to using social media, you need to be able to describe yourself, at least briefly. You may, likewise, need to write a profile, or biography, on behalf of someone else, or with the purposes of presenting yourself for work.

Though a complete biography can span all of your life and experience, an effective profile should only include the most important information. What the most important information is will depend on the purpose of the profile. You may need to write very different profiles for different contexts. For example, if you were writing a byline for a blog article on diets, you might include relevant information about your experience in health and any health-related successes you have had. You might have achieved great things in business, but it would not be relevant here. On the other hand, if you were writing for a business journal your profile should reflect your business successes, and not the elements of your life that relate to health and fitness. Both, of course, may be valuable areas of expertise, but are only relevant depending on the context of the article. If your business article related to a fitness enterprise, the biography would be different again.

The easiest way to write a profile is to start with everything that seems relevant and cut it back until the barest essentials remain. Set a word limit to help with this. Profiles should always be short and to the point, particularly for publishing credits and online profiles.

Profiles should be factual and simple. They need to be easy to follow to make your achievements and the important details clear. Profiles have a job to do, though, in selling the experience, so they should flow like a story and use language that highlights the subject matter.

Always consider the response you would like your biography to get from a reader. The purpose is usually to convince a reader that you are worth their attention, rather than to merely recite facts. Bear in mind that you must be convincing, not merely interesting. Using specific facts, figures and other details is more effective than relying on describing words. Consider the difference that precision makes in these examples:

- Leon built many houses across Essex. *(vague, not engaging)*
- Leon built 24 houses, across the towns of Brentwood, Harlow and Thurrock. *(specific details, more convincing)*
- Thelma had a fantastic, long run as a lead dancer in Moscow. *(subjective, descriptive language)*
- Thelma led the Moscow Flamingo dance troupe for 15 years. *(specific details, more neutral and therefore more convincing)*

Try to connect sentences by picking out ideas that are linked thematically. This does not always have to follow a chronological order, particularly if you are writing with limited space:

> Mr James was a successful businessman in the '80s and used that experience to open the Queen's Park Hotel in 2012. He had also studied botany during his time at university, which proved useful for tending the hotel's grounds.

In this example, the first sentence follows the theme of his professional development and the second explains his development of the grounds. Building an image in this way, you can draw out important details without telling a linear story.

23. Exam Essays

Writing for exams requires specific skills fitting to the particular format of the exam. In fact, writing well for exams is typically not a reflection of fluency, but more a case of practice. To achieve maximum marks in an exam, it is essential to satisfy its conditions, writing in a certain time-frame and presenting information in an expected manner. These skills will hopefully translate to your wider use of English, but do not assume that everyday use of English alone is enough to perform well in an exam.

Practising effective exam writing requires timed conditions. If you cannot write within a time limit outside the exam, you will find it very difficult to do so in the exam. Plan how to use your time in logical, detailed chunks. Assign time for planning and for checking your work. Both of these are as valuable for achieving marks as the time allocated for writing itself. Also plan how much time you will allow for each question, considering the marks that each question is worth. Your plans should be based on past exams and your own practice; studying examples of the exam gives you a great advantage here.

For an example of allocating time, consider a typical IELTS format:

Writing Exam – 60 minutes

Task 1 – Write a summary of a graph *(20 minutes)*

Task 2 – Write an essay discussing an opinion point *(40 minutes)*

The IELTS (International English Language Testing System) exam scores each question on the IELTS band system and combines the scores proportionately. That proportion is reflected in the allocated time. As Task 2 is worth more points, you are advised to spend more time on it. With 60 minutes available, it is possible to easily break this down using five-minute chunks:

IELTS Writing Plan

5 min	Plan Task 1
10 min	Write Task 1
5 min	Edit Task 1
5 min	Plan Task 2
10 min	Write Task 2 Paragraph 1
10 min	Write Task 2 Paragraph 2
10 min	Write Task 2 Paragraph 3
5 min	Edit Task 2

The specifics may change within a given exam (in an IELTS Task 2 question, you may need more than three paragraphs, for example), but even sticking to broad guidelines like this will ensure you have enough time to finish and edit your work. Writing to such time limits is a skill that needs to be practised and improved upon.

Similarly, selecting and presenting information in the way expected of an exam is a specific skill. It is important to use the language of the specific exam. In English exams, you will be expected to use phrases relevant to the topic or task, such as comparative language for discussing a graph or persuasive language for arguing a point. In exams for other subjects, language will be expected that is relevant to the topic: expect to use specialist language in essays, such as medical terms in medical writing or accurate names and dates in history essays. For every important exam, you will find a wealth of study material available to demonstrate what is expected.

The more specific your language is, the more efficient your writing will be, and the more convincing your points. Sometimes the most important step towards presenting the right information is knowing what you can leave out. When studying past papers, pay attention to how much detail is required for success. In the IELTS Task 1, for example, when presented with a complicated flow diagram, you can decide which points are the most important for detailed discussion, and summarise the remaining minor details, to complete the exam in time.

To achieve maximum marks in an exam, the information you present, and how you present it, should fit the expectations of the exam rather than your personal preference or style. This may be obvious in cases such as describing a process or event, but it is more complicated when you are asked to offer your opinion or make an argument. As well as writing in a neutral style, you will be expected to give a balanced argument. If asked to discuss something in positives and negatives (which most discussion essays require), to include only the positives or only the negatives, or to present a biased summary of either, will cost you marks. Remember your purpose in an exam is to score well, not to champion any particular cause.

Consider this controversial example:

> Though Adolf Hitler did a great deal of damage, he was instrumental in rebuilding Germany after the Great War.

Do you agree with the above quote?

Most people would not want to write positively about Adolf Hitler, but some consideration for his achievements is necessary here. The negatives can, of course, be presented strongly, but without first demonstrating an understanding of how the other side *could* be argued, you will lose marks.

Also remember that tone of voice is important in exams, particularly in language-based exams. Exams are typically formal, following conventions of academic writing, though more flexible when answering opinion-based questions. Generally, colloquial language, phrasal verbs, and idiomatic expressions are typically best avoided, unless they somehow fit the purpose of the exam (for example, an English essay reflecting natural use, like writing a letter to a friend).

English language exams in particular may reward a variety of correctly used phrases to demonstrate an understanding of English in use. This may seem to go against the advice throughout this book, as clear and efficient language may be scored down in exams that reward uncommon and advanced English. However, this is simply an example of when specialist and advanced language is expected and should be used accordingly. Study your exams' marking criteria to find out if demonstrating complex language use, or including certain types of language, is required.

The final, crucial step in practising for exams is getting feedback. Writing is a subjective field, but within exams there are certain criteria that must be satisfied, and in many cases only a trained eye can tell you where your exam writing needs improvement. You can read practice exam examples and the criteria for marking, but there is no substitute for someone with the right experience looking at your work and advising you on improvements.

24. Journalism

Journalistic writing usually aims to achieve two main goals: to **engage** and to **inform**. How it achieves these may depend entirely on its house style, as every publication has its own sense of identity, and on its readership.

A good way to get an idea of different journalistic styles is to compare news articles covering the same story from different publications. You may find variations in the type of language structures and vocabulary used. Particularly note how different publications can be more or less formal, and how they make efforts (or no efforts) to appear neutral. You may also find the publication's identity affects the choice of story topics, and the way different stories are approached.

The styles used by different publications are as varied as the personalities of their ideal readers, so it is essential to study a publication's style to write in a way that fits their needs. This always starts with reading the publication itself and practising writing your own articles to fit.

Matters of style in grammar, vocabulary, formatting, and punctuation are typically closely dictated within journalism. You may see a publication using deviations from typical styles, but these deviations will be laid out and consistent for that publication. This is illustrated by the flexible use of grammar seen in writing headlines, which may be quite different to everyday English but should be the same throughout all a publication's material. See **26. Headlines and Titles** for more details on this.

A useful starting point when writing journalism is to ask whether the writing is personal or impersonal. The question of perspective can inform a style. An article in the first person immediately tells us it is likely to be subjective. A first-person account offers the opportunity for editorial comment (the writer can offer their own thoughts on the topic), and gives the writer the opportunity to become an actor in the story. Such writing is common in Comment or Opinion columns, where a journalist interprets the meaning of events, rather than merely reporting them. It is also found in travel writing and long-form interviews, where the journalist's opinion of the environment and the subject are used to add context.

Otherwise, journalistic pieces are likely to be in the third person perspective voice, to give an essentially neutral report of events. The third person in journalism can still become subjective depending on the way information is presented, however, and may include adjectives that promote a certain viewpoint, without actively stating personal support. Consider the difference between the following three styles:

- When the House voted against the latest bill, it made me furious – they don't know how it affects the working man! *(first person, opinion-based)*

- The House voted against the latest bill, angering some, as it has been perceived that the views of ordinary working men have not been taken into account. *(third person, neutral and assigning opinion with the passive, avoiding agreeing with the viewpoint)*

- The House voted against the latest bill without consulting working men, an act of disregard that is now stirring anger. *(third person, demonstrating opinion by actively reporting the viewpoint as fact, with a negative label)*

As well as establishing a viewpoint, particular care must be given to how formal journalistic writing is. Some publications expect colloquial, friendly language, while others aim for more academic English. This does not necessarily relate to how neutral the text is. Informal phrases that do not necessarily convey opinion can still be used to report objectively:

- The House voted the latest bill down, causing trouble as some people claim no one's listening to the workers. *(third person, neutral and with a less formal style, avoiding assigning the viewpoint)*

Such informal language could be seen to be more subjective if perceived to treat a serious subject lightly, but otherwise it is a case of meeting readers' expectations.

To write for a specific publication, you must therefore not only consider its style but also its readership's tastes. Many publications have guidelines for positions on a range of topics, which can affect what you can and cannot write. This may relate to specific vocabulary that is restricted or encouraged, and to specific topics that are restricted or encouraged.

As a final point, despite the variations in style and potential bias, journalism is always expected to demonstrate the highest quality writing. Publications typically have a hierarchy of editors to avoid mistakes. As journalism is always public-facing, and expected to be widely read, mistakes can be damaging for a publication, and can cause readers to focus on the quality of the writing instead of the issue being discussed. Even informal or smaller publications hold the quality of writing to a high standard, within the framework their house style has established. The British tabloids, for example, are often held as a lower grade of writing, but if you read them carefully you will see that though the language may be colloquial and simple, it is carefully designed to suit its purpose.

Beyond the dual principles of writing for an audience and keeping a publication's style in mind, journalism is a very broad field that can be highly specialised. If it is a particular interest of yours, it is wise to seek additional training specifically in journalism, which will cover best practices not just in writing but in the practical areas that would inform research and, consequently, what you can write about.

25. Online Articles

When writing for online publications and larger websites, many of the same considerations apply as covered in **24. Journalism**. However, online articles can be more flexible than traditional journalism, and in many situations the house style of a website will be less formally fixed. If you write for a new website, small website, or your own website, you may have to make these style decisions yourself.

In most cases, online articles are short and direct, seldom more than 500 words long. Readers online look for easily identified summaries, such as headings and lists, so online articles are often formatted in short paragraphs using different sized fonts. Bold and italics are commonly used. Effective online article writing particularly rewards a short and simple style, as many readers merely skim articles.

Online articles tend to be less formal than traditional journalism, often using lighter language, such as colloquialisms, phrasal verbs and idioms, and personal opinion. Online articles are also rarely edited as thoroughly as traditionally published journalism, so mistakes are more common (perhaps even forgivable), though they still reflect badly on the writer (and/or the host website). The biggest difference between writing online and in traditional journalism, however, is that the emphasis has swung towards **engaging** rather than **informing** the reader. In a newspaper or magazine, it is understood that the reader is already engaged in reading your publication. Online, it is difficult to keep people's attention, so writers must employ methods to actively keep people reading.

If you can break down your articles into points with clear headings, this helps separate text on a screen. Likewise, keeping your paragraphs and sentences especially short makes them easier to follow, which encourages a reader to keep reading. It is also worth spending more time on your titles and headings than in other forms of writing, as these may be the focal points of online writing.

In general journalism, you may use a limited number of titles, and can get away with being more informative without resorting to tricks to engage the reader, but online titles are used more frequently, and are designed to entice. Consider the following article plan about a popular story from history in which explorer Henry Stanley met Dr Livingstone in Africa:

How Stanley Found Livingstone
Title 1: The Disappearance of Livingstone
Title 2: The Origins of Stanley's Expedition
Title 3: The Famous Meeting

Spread over one or two thousand words in print, this could be a perfectly acceptable article. Online, however, readers are likely to be searching for the juicy details quickly, so the story might be divided much more frequently with more enticing titles:

"Dr Livingstone, I presume?" – The True Story Behind This Phrase
Title 1: How the West Lost Livingstone
Title 2: Stranded in Zanzibar
Title 3: Henry Stanley: Journalist, Explorer, and Adventurer
Title 4: A Hundreds-Strong Expedition
Title 5: The Perils of African Exploration
Title 6: The Famous Meeting
Title 7: What Became of Livingstone?

The traditional style could be possible online, depending on the website, but more casual, energetic writing styles are increasingly common. A popular technique is to engage the reader with questions designed to inspire curiosity:

- How much do you know about Livingstone's peril?
- Did Henry Stanley invent the details of his meeting?
- Was Stanley best for the job – or the only man who'd take it?

In online article writing, this can even shift towards challenging the reader in manipulative ways, without necessarily saying what the article is about:

- Could you have survived Stanley's expedition?

Extreme examples of this are common now, and online readers are often presented with articles that exaggerate or may even falsify information. This creates a negative side to online writing:

- 92% of people don't know the true story of David Livingstone – do you?

This is commonly called **clickbait**, which is when writing (or other media) is designed entirely to get people clicking. It often uses irresistible questions and withheld information. Deliberately bad English may also be used in such articles and headings, because it draws attention to itself, for example with colloquial first-person captions.

This style of writing should be avoided, as it relies on tricks instead of good writing. It may work on occasion, but it is unlikely to be taken seriously. If you wish to be respected online, stick to the principles of effective writing to engage and inform your readership, and your work will have more long-term impact.

Once you have established a style, how do you create a typical article? Articles can vary in length, and topic, with many online examples relying on media such as pictures. For the purposes of standard written articles, however, a few basic principles can help.

Before you write anything, ask:

1. Who is the article for?
2. What do they want to know?
3. Why?

For example, the answers for a football game report might be:

1. Football fans.
2. What happened in the game / how the teams performed.
3. Because they didn't see the match and are interested in the details.

With those answers in place, you know what is important and what can be left out. In this case, you need to focus on action and results, and should use the vocabulary of football (such as *fouls*, *passes*, *goals*, etc.). The more detailed your answers here, the easier it will be to get started. If we aimed

157

this article at football fans from one particular team, we would also know how to set the tone of the report (celebrating a success / mourning a loss, how to present the atmosphere).

Following from your planning questions, you can brainstorm all the information you might present, then decide which details are the most important. Mind maps (arranging your ideas in a diagram) and brainstorms are useful, where you simply list everything you can think of.

Depending on the length of the article, aiming for three to five main points of discussion should be enough to form a logical paragraph plan. You can group your ideas under these different points. When you have a simplified structure in place, the article should have a clear direction: you will be aware of why you are writing each section, and what details each paragraph should contain.

When you are ready to start writing, the following general structure may be useful. This is not universally used, but it is a common way to approach article writing, and a good, logical starting point:

Introduction: With online articles, introductions are typically used to grab the reader's attention and generate curiosity. Try to summarise what the article will be about in a way that invites the reader to ask questions, so they will read on.

Middle/Main Content: Online, it is important to keep paragraphs short and to the point. Consider giving each major point and viewpoint its own paragraph. When presenting information, instructions, or a narrative, similarly divide information frequently for new ideas.

Conclusion: The conclusion should present the main points of the article in a clear and succinct way. Online articles typically encourage an action from the reader, so consider this when writing your final sentence. Even something as simple as inviting the reader to read another article or leave a comment can be useful.

As online introductions and conclusions act as summaries, and can be designed to directly engage, it may be easier to write these paragraphs last. Your ideas will be more fully formed after you have written your main content, so you can focus on how to effectively engage the reader with them.

26. Headlines and Titles

As publications follow specific style guidelines, newspapers, magazines, and websites often include exceptions to typical English rules. Headlines in newspapers, in particular, use different grammar rules to everyday English. This is because they are designed to be short and to attract attention.

The following eight rules are the most common variations used in headline writing, found across a range of written media, particularly online writing. These rules typically apply to journalism and other report writing (including some business writing), but are less common in formal writing, such as academic papers or formal publications like books, so do study other writing in your field to see which rules are used (or not). Where permitted, though, these tips can work to create more striking headlines and titles.

1. Use present simple tense for past events

The present tense is quick and current, and helps emphasise the action happening, rather than its completion:

- Parliament Confirms New Stray Dog Policy
- Lion Escapes Zoo

For the result of an action, or something that has been specifically completed, perfect tenses are used; for changing events, the present continuous may be used. Both tenses often use participles alone, as discussed below.

2. Leave out auxiliary verbs

With perfect, progressive, and passive structures, auxiliary verbs are not necessary in headlines. This makes some headlines appear to be in the past simple, when actually the headlines have a perfect or passive meaning.

Changing events are represented by the present participle on its own:

- New Policy Decided by Parliament
  (new policy has been decided/was decided by Parliament)
- Lion Escapes Zoo – Ten Killed
  (ten people have been killed/were killed)
- Four Stranded in Sudden Flood
  (four people have been stranded/were stranded)

3. Use infinitives for future events

A future time is not necessary to demonstrate the future tense in headlines, as an infinitive form can demonstrate the future:

- Parliament to Vote on Hunting Ban
- President to Visit France for Further Talks

4. Leave out articles *(a, an, the)*

Articles and determiners can be omitted in headlines, unless they are important to aid understanding:

- Prime Minister Hikes Alps for Charity
  (the Prime Minister hiked the Alps)
- Man Releases Rabid Dog in Park
  (a man released a rabid dog in a/the park)

5. Leave out "to be"

As with auxiliary verbs, **to be** may be omitted from headlines, as an adjective or other describing phrase can clearly imply a state:

- Residents Unhappy About New Road
  (residents are unhappy)
- Victim Satisfied with Court Decision
  (victim is satisfied)

6. Leave out "to say"

Reported speech is usually represented by a colon, or a hyphen, with the subject introduced with *on...*:

- Mr Jones: "They Won't Take My House!"
- Bush on Iraqi Invasion: "This Aggression Will Not Stand."

Other verbs such as *comment, tell, argue, announce, shout*, etc. can be left out, unless the act of speaking needs emphasising, for instance to demonstrate a promise or official policy:

- Warlord Decrees "Peace by Spring."

7. Replace conjunctions with punctuation

As with reporting speech, commas, colons, semi-colons, hyphens, and so on can replace all conjunctions, or some joining verbs, to join clauses:

- Police Arrest Serial Killer – Close Case on Abductions
- Fire in Bakery: Hundreds of Loaves Lost

Commas may also be used to join nouns, though this is more common in American English than British English.

- Man Kills 5, Self

8. Use figures for numbers

Using figures in a headline is more likely to catch the reader's attention:

- 9 Dead in Glue Catastrophe
- 7 Days to Christmas – Shoppers Go Mad

These eight tips can be useful, but use them with caution. Grammar variations can lead to ambiguous headlines, as many words are implied and not written, so be careful when applying them to make sure that your headline can be understood. It should have a single, clear meaning.

Different vocabulary may also be used in headlines. Concise verbs which are not common in general English are often used, such as *bid*, *vow,* and *spark*. Additional style issues to consider for certain publications include use of Title Case (as explained in **15.6 Capital Letters**) and commas, though these should be covered by your overall considerations for the house style.

27. Business Writing

Business writing can refer to a wide range of texts, including correspondence, reports, publications, presentations, and more. Though business texts can have many uses, they share certain common principles.

Business writing is typically formal, like academic writing. Likewise, technical terms are expected in business writing, when you know your intended audience will understand such words. Otherwise, the best practice for business writing is to keep things as direct and simple as possible, for maximum clarity and accuracy. Mistakes in business communications can be very costly, so it is especially important to focus on accuracy here. You may not have dedicated editors, as in journalism or other publications; if possible, get someone else to read your writing. Even if it is an informal check from a colleague, a second opinion is invaluable during the editing process.

Business writing is typically neutral, particularly when it comes to reports, though public-facing writing may have purposes more in line with marketing (as covered next in **28. Copywriting**). Depending on the context, business writing may require the active or passive voice, as there will be times when the actor is important (such as when taking responsibility or making a commitment) and times when the actor is not important (such as when discussing general trends and the results of activities):

- Global IT laid new phone lines throughout the neighbourhood, increasing connectivity. *(assigning responsibility to a specific company)*
- New phone lines were laid throughout the neighbourhood, increasing connectivity for local businesses by 25%. *(focusing on the impact rather than the actor)*

The perspective used for business writing will also depend on your context and style. Some companies consistently write in the third person, others in the first, and some use a combination depending on the situation.

163

This also applies to vocabulary and certain flexible areas of grammar and punctuation, and is particularly important for specialist terms and abbreviations. House style guides should provide guidance on all of these areas for a particular company, and if such styles are not formally covered it is worth checking particular styles with a ranking member of the company. This connects to an overriding principle that business writing is, above all, typically collaborative. Unless you are working for yourself, consulting with colleagues is essential for consistency.

27.1 Business Vocabulary

Business English includes vocabulary not seen elsewhere, which can be necessary to refer to specific business practices or company-specific products and concepts. Many general business terms with less specific purposes are also used purely to communicate within the sphere of business. Such language is often referred to (negatively) as **business jargon**.

Business jargon is often used to create a professional or important appearance, but if it has no other purpose then simpler, clearer language would be more appropriate. Specialist vocabulary is only necessary when it creates an immediate understanding that other words cannot communicate. Knowing the difference between ineffective jargon and essential business language is a question of studying the vocabulary and asking:

1. Does this word or phrase convey a unique and specific meaning?
2. Is there a simpler or clearer way to say this?

Business vocabulary is diverse, and dependent on different industries, so it is impossible to present any comprehensive list of words which are useful, and words which are not, but a few examples can illustrate the difference:

- Our wireless kettles set the **benchmark** for the **product line**.

In this example, *benchmark* and *product line* indicate specific meanings that would be hard to replace with anything simpler. In fact, searching for more common alternatives would make this sentence more confusing. Words like *benchmark* and *product line* are common enough to be easily understood in a business context. (Though note that such vocabulary may be undesirable in public-facing writing, such as advertising copy.) Compare with:

- Management requests that all employees **think outside the box** to complete the **actionables** from the Midsummer Report.

Think outside the box is an example of clichéd business vocabulary, sometimes referred to as **management speak**. Such language can lead to negative responses because it identifies the speaker or writer as someone who relies on unnecessary jargon. The problem with business vocabulary like this (as with clichés in general) is that it avoids specifics. Using abstract ideas and longer phrases makes sentences more confusing, which is the opposite purpose of specialist vocabulary. In this case (as with similar phrases like *blue-sky thinking* or *squaring the circle*), to *think outside the box* does not clearly define an idea. It indirectly encourages *creative thinking* or *original thinking*, both of which phrases which make the same point in a clearer way. More effective still would be writing that moves the idea in a specific direction. A practical alternative would be: "all employees *think of two or three new ideas*". Asking employees to *think of ideas* creates the same point without risking confusion or sounding lofty and patronising.

Actionables is a more subtle case. It is the sort of fashionable business vocabulary, or **buzzword**, that has emerged to represent a specific meaning (*items that can be acted on*), though it can be argued that a more common word could convey the same meaning (e.g. *tasks*). For general use, a simpler option is clearer and does not create any hint of management speak, though depending on personal preference and style, *actionables* could be justified, as it refers to a specific concept. The problem with words like *actionables*, which have a specific business use, is that when they are not considered necessary their purposes appear to be aesthetic. In some contexts, jargon-dense writing may be used to win the respect of the reader who enjoys such language; in most cases, aiming to convey a clear message is better.

Though more can be done to edit this example, just by focusing on these two pieces of business vocabulary it is possible to write a simpler and more accessible sentence:

- Management requests that all employees think of two or three ideas to complete the tasks from the Midsummer Report.

It can be tempting to use jargon to fit in with others in a business context, and this is a consideration that must be made on a case by case basis. Mostly, using only the language that provides clear and specific meanings will ensure clearer and accurate writing. If you are communicating or collaborating with others that use and expect business jargon, then such jargon may be effective for the purposes of that writing. In general, however, try not to adopt bad practices that others use.

28. Copywriting

Copywriting, mostly associated with marketing, is a part of writing for businesses, but its particular purpose is to generate a response, making it very different in practice. Copywriting is often tested and based on statistics rather than personal preference, though overall styles may be defined. This means that the actual wording of writing for marketing purposes may be decided by how people respond to it, not by the principles of what is considered to be good writing.

If your audience responds better to long sentences than short sentences, long sentences are better. If your audience responds better to complicated or abstract words, they are better than simple and clear words. The same could be said of other fields, of course, but copywriting typically has the mechanisms in place to produce such analysis.

For the most part, this is simply putting theory into ruthless practice: throughout this book, I have said that the best writing is the most appropriate for the purpose, and the audience. In copywriting, there are simply ways to test the most effective writing – by splitting variations of emails for different audiences, for example, or by running adverts in different regions, and analysing link clicks or sales.

This is fine for dictating style issues, but it is important to recognise when the results undermine accepted rules of English. If incorrect punctuation produces a better result, for example, it may be due to a misunderstanding. Genuine errors in English, after all, are those that make a message unclear, so if the tested results go against the most accepted rules of English, the writing may actually be misleading (and even if not, such inaccuracies may create a bad image for a business).

Before you get to the stage of testing your writing, you can start with the principles highlighted throughout this book. Aim for language that is clear and simple, and use specialist language only when it is appropriate for your audience. Use exceptions rarely to avoid them losing their impact. Read widely to understand what your readers expect and already know.

Copywriting can be the reverse of formal business and academic writing. Generally, marketing copy needs to be informal, direct, and accessible, as the purpose is to engage and persuade rather than to present a company or idea professionally. Exactly how informal your marketing copy can be depends on the market, but generally light, friendly copywriting is more effective at engaging people. The exceptions are in industries where the subject matter is necessarily serious and customers are searching for security and assurance; for example, in finance or funeral care. Even in these cases, though, copywriting should be aimed at making a personal connection.

With this in mind, copywriting is one of the main areas where the second person perspective is used, particularly to ask questions of the reader, or to try and transport them to a different place. Emotional language can also be used, particularly if it generates curiosity, urgency, fear, or excitement. Open questions are useful for this:

- Which of these sofas will change your life? *(the curiosity of what this product can do for you)*
- Can you afford <u>not</u> to read this book? *(the fear of missing out)*
- If you like chocolate, you'll love McChoco Lollipops. *(the excitement of a new way to enjoy an existing passion)*

Copywriting can be a very creative area. You can experiment with flamboyant language and broken sentences, for example. Also consider the flexible rules of writing headlines (see **26. Headlines and Titles**), and take guidance from fiction and storytelling. Often, the same elements that make a good story engaging work for marketing, too, including the principle of Show Don't Tell (which is covered in **31.1 Show Don't Tell**).

Writing to produce a response goes beyond these principles, however. It is a science that has been well served by a number of excellent books. The techniques in style guides such as *Elements of Style* (Strunk and White, 1999) help produce accurate English, while books on copywriting craft can offer tested techniques for the business of selling through writing. *Writing that Works* (Roman & Raphaelson, 2000) is a good introduction to the art of business writing, while Andy Maslen's books, such as *Write to Sell* (2009), give scientific and accessible advice on writing to generate a response.

29. Cover Letters

Everyone communicating in English writes cover letters, whether for work, school, or proposals of any kind. Whatever the purpose, cover letters can be guided by common principles for how much information you include, what details you include, and how formal you are.

Cover letters are mostly under a page long. They can usually be broken down into a standard structure:

1. Salutation
2. Introductory statement/paragraph
3. Summary of proposal
4. Relevant additional information (often more detail about the sender)
5. Closing statement and valediction

A cover letter should only include information specific to your proposal, and only enough information as that proposal requires. Anything extra will dilute your message.

Do not write too much, in general, and only include essential information. A cover letter should not tell the reader everything about you and it should not be used to demonstrate your wide range of language skills. Overlong or overcomplicated cover letters can be distracting or confusing, and run the risk of putting a reader off.

Remember that the main aim of a cover letter is to capture the reader's attention. Even if you have, for example, a dozen examples of relevant experience, these can be summarised, with only the two or three most important points highlighted. Your reader can only process so much information at once, after all.

The following two examples give an idea of how the above structure can be elaborated, in a very brief form. Both examples are particularly short, but this may be as much information as a cover letter requires.

Example 1

1. Salutation:

   Dear Mr Walters,

2. Introduction:

   Please find attached my entry for the *Better Weather Anthology* competition, a 500-word article entitled "What's in the Water".

3. Proposal:

   "What's in the Water" documents the increase of waste off the coast of Norfolk, drawing on data from the Local Environmental Agency and from the RSPB. It shows that levels of pollution have risen by 42% in the last five years, because of shipping channels.

4. Additional information:

   I am a freelance writer with a background as an environmental scientist. I have written for BBC Magazine and my book, *Greener than Grass*, won the Regional Award for Awareness. I write on matters that demand action, and am particularly eager to raise awareness about this issue.

5. Closing statement and valediction:

   Please let me know if you require anything else from me. I look forward to hearing from you.

   Yours sincerely,

   Clarice Mayweather

Example 2

1. Salutation:

   Dear Sir or Madam,

2. Introduction:

   I am writing to submit my resume for the position of Head Chef, as seen in the London Gazette's classified advert.

3. Proposal:

   I am a fully qualified chef with ten years' catering experience. I worked in the Hilton Hotel and The Blue Boat Restaurant, and was awarded the Best Chef Award in 2014.

4. Additional information:

   In addition to catering, I have experience in management, as I ran a supply shop in Littlehampton, and am a keen fisherman, making me particularly enthusiastic about seafood.

5. Closing statement and valediction:

   My CV is attached. Please let me know if you require anything else from me, and I look forward to hearing from you.

   Yours faithfully,

   Bill Bronson

While you may be as brief as these two examples, be sure to always provide all the information required. Before sending any cover letter, check for any special requirements from the recipient. Some cover letters may require information in a list format, with specific details to be included. Be guided by the instructions you are given; cover letters that fail to follow instructions, no matter how effectively written, may not be read.

29.1 The Tone of a Cover Letter

A cover letter should always be polite and respectful. Avoid the temptation to stand out by doing something unusual with your cover letter, such as using odd language, structures, or layouts. The content of your letter is what most readers are after, and creative cover letters typically distract from the information you provide. You may see rare examples of creative cover letters than work, but these are always exceptions. The most effective cover letters present the most appropriate and impressive content in a professional way.

Though being polite and respectful is a good start, the quickest route to engaging a reader (or failing to engage them) is by connecting on a personal level (or failing to connect). Connecting with your reader comes from demonstrating relevant understanding of who you are addressing, starting with their name. Try to include a sentence, or at least a statement, that shows you know who you are writing to, and indicate the letter is specifically for them. Give an idea of why you are writing to them in particular, and why you are a good fit. Keep it short, offering just enough to make a connection:

> I've been eager to join your school since my cousin attended in 2009, and my ambition to attend myself has pushed me to achieve my current grades.

After this point, cover letters should be formal. Avoid colloquialisms, irrelevant personal details, and overly friendly language or inappropriate punctuation (for example, exclamation points). Formal language has become more relaxed in emails, but until your recipient invites a more relaxed tone it is safer to be polite. You are unlikely to cause problems using formal language, but you may be seen as less serious using informal language.

That said, keep a personal and friendly touch in mind. Use the lighter suggestions for formal language, and avoid complicated structures or vocabulary. For example, active sentences will work better in cover letters than passive sentences, keeping things direct and efficient (*I qualified at Nottingham*, NOT *My degree was earned at Nottingham*).

30. Emails

Writing is a part of everyday life on the internet. With everyone using email to communicate, the styles available for writing emails are as diverse as there are people. As email is so common, it has become less formal than writing for publications or letter writing. Informal salutations and valedictions are common in email, even for more formal purposes, such as addressing a stranger. The language used in email is often lighter and more casual than in other areas of writing, and standards for accuracy may be lower.

As flexible as email is, however, there is no harm in being clear, polite and respectful in your writing. When dealing with formal contacts, such as strangers, business associates, and professionals, or when sending a cover letter as an email, formal salutations and conventions will not look out of place, so a good rule is to start formal and allow your reader's response to dictate how you form future emails. This applies to other aspects of your writing in emails, too, including the complexity of your vocabulary and sentence structures.

30.1 Opening and Closing an Email

How you start or end an email depends on your relationship to the recipient. People open and close emails in ways entirely suited to their personalities, so do not be surprised to see a range from very brief to very formal language used in salutations and valedictions.

If in doubt, sticking to conventional methods is a safe bet. You can always adjust your style later, according to the situation. For example, if you send an initial email addressed *Dear Dr Hiller* and receive the reply *Hi Janet!* your following email might be lighter: *Hi Dr Hiller*.

Valedictions in emails can be particularly diverse. The standard farewells are used, but so are countless alternative valedictions, including well-wishing and simple closing statements, such as *All the best!* or *Hope to hear from you soon,* followed by a name. You may also find conventions entirely abandoned in emails, with some people writing without any introduction or farewell, as you might with a text message. Again, observe these practices but aim for something more standardised yourself.

30.2 Email Subject Lines

An area of email that stands out from other areas of letter writing is having to title your email in the subject line.

There are many ways to approach email subject lines. Some people treat them as reference points, others like headlines. Whatever the case, it's best to be short and descriptive, without being too dramatic or using marketing language. The following guidelines refer to subject lines for everyday emails, such as for correspondence and information. When it comes to promotional emails, such as for selling a product, the techniques can be more diverse and rely more on the principles that make headlines and copywriting successful.

The simplest way to produce an everyday subject line is to approach it the same way you would a chapter title. Can your email, or overall message, be summed up in one or two words? Consider (a) the most important theme in the email and (b) if there is an important point to highlight. For instance, for an email complaining about the conditions of a washroom, the theme is a *complaint* and the important point is the *washroom conditions*, so the subject line could be: *Washroom conditions complaint*. With an email requesting information about new timetables for teaching history, the theme is *timetables*, the point is that they are *for history teachers*: *History teachers' timetables*.

You may wish to include important names, titles, positions, and reasons for writing to add extra detail to such subjects:

- John Smith's lesson plan
- Managing Director's Report
- Rat infestation query

The most important words should come first, as your reader may see the message on a mobile device that does not display the full subject (or they may only read the first few words). Consider the subject, *Important update about the new time for the grammar class on Thursday*. If a reader only saw *Important update about the...*, the subject is not clear and may be ignored. Better would be: *Thursday's Grammar Class – New Time*.

Any word that does not highlight an important point of the email should be removed. As with headlines, covered in **26. Headlines and Titles**, some everyday grammar rules may be ignored in an email subject line. Words only there to perform a grammatical function can be cut. Adjectives, adverbs, prepositions, and articles can often be removed, as well as many question words, possessives, and verbs. Exactly what is important depends on your email, but always be aware that the fewer words the better:

- Your schedule for the weekend trip
  → Weekend trip schedule
- Question regarding the new English classroom's heating
  → New classroom heating question
- What documents you must remember to submit for your coursework next week
  → Necessary coursework documents

If the reader needs to find your email in future, they may use email searches and filters, so consider what they would search for. Use distinct words that do not have multiple meanings or could form parts of other words, such as *invoice* instead of *bill*; use specific dates instead of relative times (*April 13th* instead of *next Tuesday*); and use names instead of titles. For example, *This month's website bill* gives an unclear time with unspecific words that would be difficult to find in a search. *February Website Hosting Invoice* uses searchable words for a date, product/service, and topic.

31. Storytelling

The language used for telling stories in English can be as varied as the writer wishes, ranging from very efficient, simple language to very complex, experimental language. If you are in the early stages of writing in English, it is worth aiming for a middle ground, working with conventional styles, as extremely simple creative writing requires a great deal of discipline, while experimental writing requires expertise to avoid perceived mistakes.

The tips in Part 1 introduced the basics of achieving conventionally effective writing, such as planning, simplicity, and choosing your descriptive language, tenses, and perspectives carefully. This section looks at some considerations specifically useful for creative storytelling.

Stories may apply structures and themes that are not relevant in other forms of writing. These ideas can require whole books to explore, such as the famous conventions for mythological story structure detailed in *The Hero with a Thousand Faces* (Joseph Campbell, 2008). In brief, these structures provide conventions for a plotted arc for a character to follow, including developments at particular points in the story.

Thematic considerations, too, can dictate the sort of language you use and how you introduce particular information. These ideas are not specific to English language stories, but apply to storytelling in general. It is useful to consider common genre ideas and how they affect language, which you can do through studying examples.

As writing stories is typically the area of inventive ideas, descriptive language in storytelling can be more creative than in other areas. A good starting point for this is mastering techniques such as **similes** (a comparison stating one thing is like another) and **metaphors** (a comparison describing one thing as another). As with other describing words and phrases, these should be used in a limited fashion, for the best effect, and should always be appropriate. Make sure that your references are appropriate to the context, too.

A historical romance, for example, should not include language that refers to modern technology:

- The peasants met on the castle bridge in moonlight the shade of a halogen bulb. *(very inappropriate)*
- The peasants met on the castle bridge in moonlight the shade of an alabaster vase. *(appropriate to the setting)*

31.1 Show Don't Tell

A tip that appears more in writing stories than any other form of writing is **Show Don't Tell**. This is as effective in storytelling as Keep It Simple is in general writing. Showing instead of telling means demonstrating details rather than stating them:

- Looking at her made him happy. *(tell)*
- Looking at her gave him a warm feeling in his belly. *(show)*

This can be applied to all areas of a story, not just description, and it does not necessarily mean you need to show an event or action. Additional information can be demonstrated through the ways characters talk to each other or through physical traits, without directly stating the details to the reader. In the examples below, both describing the same scene, almost all of the information told in the first, longer passage, can be interpreted in the simple second example:

- Vera held out the USB drive with reluctance. She wasn't sure if the man could be trusted; even if she handed over the files they wanted, they might not release her friend Tim.
- Vera held out the USB drive but her hand wavered. "You promise to let Tim go?"

The principle of **Show Don't Tell** works because efficient language in storytelling encourages readers to use their imagination and infer and interpret certain details. This makes the writing both quicker to read and more engaging.

31.2 Genres in Fiction

Genre in writing refers to different conventions of tone, content, and style that are expected in relation to certain texts. Genres are not only found in fiction, as other subjects in Part 2 could be referred to as non-fiction genres (such as *journalism* and *academic books*), but the major genre conventions for fiction create a particularly diverse field to consider.

This section briefly looks at common fiction genres and how they impact writing decisions, to give an idea for how to think about genre in general. There are many more different categories available than are covered here. Also remember that many works of fiction cross over different genres (for example, fantasy romances or crime thrillers) and may combine various elements from the main genre conventions.

31.2.1 Literary Fiction

Literary fiction refers to writing developed and received critically, like an art-form. Literary fiction typically explores deep themes, such as emotional, political or other reflections. It is often slower in pace and more distinct in style than other genres.

By its nature, literary fiction can break rules and conventions and be experimental, and can include various forms of genre fiction where the writing is considered to go beyond the usual conventions. Plot structure is less important in literary fiction, where emotional development and creative use of language may be more appreciated.

Some literary fiction includes other genre fiction that has found appeal outside its genre, most likely due to the effectiveness of its style or themes. For example, Margaret Atwood's *The Handmaid's Tale* fits the genre of dystopian fiction (a sub-genre of sci-fi), but is widely considered to be literary fiction for its well-handled themes and skilful writing.

31.2.2 Romance

Romance fiction typically follows the relationships of two or more main characters, with a romantic climax; for example, with a couple united or separated. The theme of romance should be present throughout, with actions and scenes impacting the relationship between the key characters. Romance stories are usually moral, rewarding good behaviour and punishing bad behaviour. A happy ending is often expected, but not always; a key example of a diverging romance is Shakespeare's *Romeo and Juliet*.

Suiting the theme, the language of romance stories often includes detail about the characters' thoughts and feelings. Romance stories can occur in any time and place, with the genre spanning historical, fantasy, and paranormal fiction as well as contemporary stories. In all cases, romance and relationships are the driving force of the story.

Romance is often connected to erotic fiction, but a theme of romance does not necessarily provide an excuse for excessive sexual content. This will depend on the particular sub-genre and audience.

31.2.3 Crime and Mystery

Crime fiction usually involves a mystery that must be solved. Most often this relates to a crime in the early stages of the story that is not explained until the end, such as with a murder mystery.

Crime or mystery stories typically follow the main character's journey towards gathering enough information to solve the crime, with events either moving that story forward or creating and resolving additional twists and mysterious sub-plots.

As crime/mystery fiction relies on a reader's curiosity, the genre benefits from a very close narrative style, often in the first person or third person limited. To create maximum tension and intrigue, these stories relate to dark themes such as murder, and often have gritty settings with flawed main characters (such as an alcoholic detective). The journey to solving a crime can be violent and the language crude, though some of the most popular crime writers deal with dark themes without using bad language, and there are popular lighter mystery stories that deal with less extreme themes.

31.2.4 Science Fiction

Science fiction covers a great number of genres that may be more broadly referred to as speculative fiction: creative writing which presents an unreal world (or universe) based on realistic possibilities. This includes futuristic stories with imagined new technology, but may also cover contemporary, historical, or otherworldly settings.

The main convention that marks science fiction is presenting these unreal elements in a realistic way, so it typically uses formal language and academic themes. The tone of voice may be irreverent and the stories informal (including rough characters, for example), but it is rare for science fiction not to have at least some element of scientifically discussed themes. There are, of course, variations of this, for example with humorous sci-fi, but the scientific concepts will still be presented as plausible.

Otherwise, sci-fi is an incredibly broad category that can include stories spanning any other genre. The conventions of the story itself may, for example, reflect the saga of a fantasy, the emotional language of a romance, or the mystery of a crime novel. The key to making the elements of science fiction successful is to relate the imagined technology in a way that is both seamless and critical to the story.

31.2.5 Fantasy

Fantasy broadly refers to any fiction with unreal elements that are not necessarily based on real-world ideas or technology.

The main difference between fantasy and science fiction is that things are possible in fantasy without roots in reality, whereas science fiction is typically limited to the realistically possible. Fantasy can therefore include magic and other ideas that cannot be explained within our world. As fantasy often relates to new and unusual worlds, it is common to find elaborately descriptive writing in fantasy, with longer stories that can more fully explore alternative realities.

Although fantasy does not need to be realistic, it should be considered real within the story's world. Avoid using language that highlights fantasy elements as strange (or otherwise undermines them), unless it is relevant to the story (for example, an outsider encountering the unknown).

31.2.6 Horror

Horror stories are designed to be distressing, either through psychological or physical horror, or a combination of the two. In horror, the plot often revolves around survival, with explanations or other goals secondary.

Descriptions, relationships, and character building, unless relating to the horror itself, may be more superficial and simpler in horror than other genres, with the emphasis on atmosphere and action. Horror often has unhappy endings and more graphic language, including violence and cursing (though such elements are not always necessary, and some of the most effective classical horror stories use limited description and inoffensive language).

Perspective is important in horror, as the characters must frequently be in danger. While the first person can give us insights into a character's fear, it is more difficult to build a sense of danger when we know they are telling the story, so the choice must be made carefully.

31.2.7 Thriller

Thrillers are often connected to crime and mystery novels, as a common driving force of the thriller is unravelling a secret. The typical convention in thriller writing is for the main character to be put in an uncomfortable and unexplained situation, with the resolution coming from solving a mystery and facing the foe responsible.

Thriller fiction can span various sub-genres, particularly crime and spy stories, and can have a lot in common with horror as they both explore dangerous situations. However, while horror puts an emphasis on survival and has no requirement to explain its events, thrillers are usually more concerned with mystery and escape.

By their nature, thrillers benefit from shorter, simpler language for a faster pace, and often include more action than description.

31.2.8 Humour

Humour in fiction can take any form, and is often found as part of a wider genre rather than as a main genre itself. In a dedicated humour story, however, the focus is on creating entertaining situations and using amusing language throughout, rather than simply adding humour to a story driven by other conventions.

The result is that humour fiction may be more farcical and absurd than other genres, and often includes language precisely designed for jokes, such as unexpected vocabulary or stark variations in grammar or style. Humour often relies on a particular tone, dependent on a character or narrator's particular sense of humour, which will continually affect choices of vocabulary and narrative voice.

31.2.9 Short Story

Short stories can be written in any genre, following the same genre conventions. They do belong in a genre of their own, too, however, as short stories of all genres share similar traits, most particularly in how they start and finish. Short stories naturally have to create their backstory in a limited space, so they often open the story late, either inferring or omitting detail. They also often end with a twist. Though it is not always the case, readers of short stories typically expect a surprise at the end.

Short stories can be as long as you choose. With the rise of the internet and more reading done on the move, **flash fiction** is becoming popular, with stories told in a page, a paragraph, a sentence, or even a phrase. Short story challenges, such as competitions based on word limits, are a good way to practice very efficient language.

Approaching such stories, however, requires some bending of the rules of language, which may lead to grammar variations. It is best to aim to have fun and be creative with short stories, then check over your work, and ideally get the opinion of a friend or keen reader before sharing your story more widely.

32. Social Media and Texts

Social media and text messaging is a rapidly evolving area which has writing at its heart. The English used online has evolved equally rapidly to meet the demands of platforms like Facebook and Twitter, with social media rewarding short and direct messages designed to grab attention. Fortunately, the same tips found throughout this book are as true in social media as they are anywhere else: clear and simple language will help you stick to limited word counts and present the most accessible messages online.

There are practices to watch out for when writing on social media platforms, however, which you may encounter other writers using. The first is the use of unconventional abbreviations, either in the wide range of acronyms used for commonly understood ideas (such as *LOL* for *laughing out loud*), or colloquial words that might have only been found in spoken English before. Being exposed to informal writing from all over the world, you may also find word usage and unconventional grammar that is not found in dictionaries or textbooks. In some cases this is merely regional English, being used flexibly by different people as it always has been, but in other cases this language has emerged through online communities. The method of understanding is no different to writing in any other field, however; read widely and you will get an idea of how particular words and phrases are used, no matter how unusual they may seem.

To a certain degree, writing online is more relaxed, as accuracy is less expected, particularly in more light-hearted social media spheres. However, it is important to remember that what you post online is often public and recorded. You want to present yourself in the best possible light, at all times, as the things you write may be read in many years' time, so do try to maintain high standards.

For the most effective communication, always try to understand where other writers come from, and who you are writing for. As with all writing, start with the conventions that work – being clear, simple and accurate – and as you move towards fluency in social media, pay close attention to the conventions being used on your chosen platform. Even if you don't find many variations in language, you are bound to find new vocabulary and new conventions that you need to continually study, as these concepts will continue to change.

As social media is a rapidly changing area, it is worth noting that the fundamentals of English writing can be affected by trends and innovations in the media being used. Text messages and communication through other, short-form platforms, may lead to abbreviated language with unique and unusual greetings and farewells (including, for example, the use of initials or a kiss **(x)** to signify the end of a message).

The use of images is also an important aspect of social media, as images become more readily available and easily shared. Images can take the place of entire messages on social media, for example through the use of emojis or animated GIFs to demonstrate a reaction.

Finally, punctuation rules may be relaxed or even heavily modified depending on the social media platform. Some online platforms restrict punctuation use, so you may find the available punctuation is used creatively. You may also find text with no punctuation, for example when people write with **hashtags**. Hashtags **(#)** are widely used to create a label that expresses a topic, category, or some kind of commentary to accompany a message or other media. The text following a hashtag, no matter how long, usually has no punctuation, meaning many words can run together:

- Watch out for hashtags #withlotsofwordswrittentogether

Afterword

Writing is a skill that takes years to master, in any language, and this book can only ever be an introduction to the methods you can use to improve in that skill. It is designed to get you thinking, rather than to guide you in exactly what you need to do.

My main goal is to move you in the right direction. The concepts that you may have found repeated throughout this book are there, again and again, for a reason: simplicity, clarity, and understanding your audience are the guiding principles of effective writing. Aim for the most appropriate writing for your purposes and you will be on the path to success.

For almost every chapter and topic in this book, there are huge amounts of additional material that can be studied, though of course there is no substitute for the practice you will get from wider reading and writing for your own purposes. By all means check some of the books in my **Recommended Reading** list, attend courses, and work with tutors or writing groups. Above all, though, read examples of what you would like to write, and challenge yourself to produce something similar. Through such active learning, you will establish and perfect your own writing voice.

As a continual student of English myself, I also encourage you to question the contents of this book. In many cases this book covers my particular thinking about writing, which can often, as we know, be a matter of style. I'm always open to considering the alternatives. Do get in touch if anything particularly works, or doesn't work, for you, I can be reached at: **phil@englishlessonsbrighton.co.uk**

If you found this book helpful, please leave a review online to help others find it. You can also sign up to my mailing list at:

www.englishlessonsbrighton.co.uk

to learn about my other upcoming books, and to receive free learning material.

Recommended Reading

Reference Books

The Chicago Manual of Style (University of Chicago Press, 17th ed., 2017)
The Elements of Style, by William Strunk Jr. and E.B. White (Pearson, 4th ed., 1999)
The Merriam-Webster Dictionary (Merriam-Webster, Inc., New edition, 2016)
The New Fowler's Modern English Usage, by H.W. Fowler (edited by R.W. Birchfield, Oxford University Press, 3rd ed., 1996)
New Hart's Rules: The Oxford Style Guide (edited by Anne Waddingham, Oxford University Press, 2nd edition, 2014)
New Oxford Dictionary for Writers and Editors (compiled by R.M. Ritter, Oxford University Press, Revised edition, 2014)

Books on Writing and Language

Eats, Shoots & Leaves: The Zero Tolerance Approach to Punctuation, by Lynne Truss (Avery, Reprint ed., 2006)
Ernest Hemingway on Writing (edited by Larry Phillips, Touchstone, 1999)
The Hero with a Thousand Faces, by Joseph Campbell (New World Library, 3rd ed., 2008)
The Mother Tongue: English and How It Got That Way, by Bill Bryson (William Morrow Paperbacks, Reissue ed., 1990)
On Writing: A Memoir of the Craft, by Stephen King (Scribner, Anniversary ed., 2010)
Wired for Story, by Lisa Cron (Ten Speed Press, 2012)
Write to Sell, by Andy Maslen (Marshall Cavendish Corporation, 2nd ed., 2009)
Writing that Works: How to Communicate Effectively in Business, by Kenneth Roman and Joel Raphaelson (Collins Reference, 3rd ed., 2000)

Available Online

Elmore Leonard's Rules for Writers, by Elmore Leonard (*The Guardian*, 2010)
https://www.theguardian.com/books/2010/feb/24/elmore-leonard-rules-for-writers

English Irregular Verbs List (Wikipedia)
http://en.wikipedia.org/wiki/English_irregular_verbs#List

Interactive Phonemic Charts, created by Adrian Underhill (Macmillan English)
http://www.macmillanenglish.com/pronunciation/interactive-phonemic-charts

Oxford Learner's Dictionaries (Oxford University Press)
https://www.oxfordlearnersdictionaries.com

Oxford Living Dictionaries (Oxford University Press)
https://en.oxforddictionaries.com

Politics and the English Language, by George Orwell (1946)
http://www.george-orwell.org/Politics_and_the_English_Language/0.html

Spelling, from Cambridge Dictionary's *English Grammar Today,* by Ronald Carter, Michael McCarthy, Geraldine Mark, and Anne O'Keeffe (Cambridge University Press)
http://dictionary.cambridge.org/grammar/british-grammar/writing/spelling

Split Infinitives (Wikipedia)
https://en.wikipedia.org/wiki/Split_infinitive

Acknowledgements

This book would not have been possible without help from my many students, who for many years have made me think about the questions I have attempted to answer here. I have been especially pushed to explain unusual things by my longest term students Pawel Leszkowicz and Loan Do. I have also been encouraged to work on this by the wonderful correspondence I receive from students and teachers all over the world via the ELB site and mailing list, and these same people have helped root out any niggling problems in the final book. In particular, thanks to Andre Bianconi, Alexander Pyvovarov, Dmitris Tsigkenis, Malcolm Maccallum, Mark Lee, and Nasir Chem.

The whole contents of the ELB site and my books are also in debt to my wife, Marta, who has always encouraged me to produce more learning material, and has sat through many hours of testing my books. Special thanks is also due to my editor Caroline Hynds, who did a wonderful job of keeping the book consistent and sensible.

Also by Phil Williams

The English Tenses Practical Grammar Guide

Quickly discover the many uses of the English tenses. How do English speakers use two tenses to mean the same thing? Why do the rules not always apply?

This comprehensive guide to the usage patterns of all 12 aspects of the English language covers all the rules and grammatical forms. The English Tenses: Practical Grammar Guide is ideal as either an accompaniment to core texts or as a full self-study guide. It introduces the reader to flexible uses of the English tenses, with simple, easy-to-follow explanations, colourful examples and enlightening comparisons.

Word Order in English Sentences

*Want to know what subject-verb-object **really** means? Unsure about where to place your adverbs? Need to rearrange sentences confidently?*

A complete foundation in word order and sentence structure for the English language, Word Order in English Sentences can be used both for reference and as a full self-study guide. From basic rules through to the many considerations of adverbial phrases, prepositions and complex sentences, with exercises in between, this grammar guide contains everything you need for a strong understanding of how sentences are put together.

The rules and patterns for forming and reforming phrases and sentences are all presented with easy-to-follow explanations, clear examples and exercises to test understanding. With his engaging style, Phil Williams takes you beyond the basics, making flexible and advanced English accessible to all.